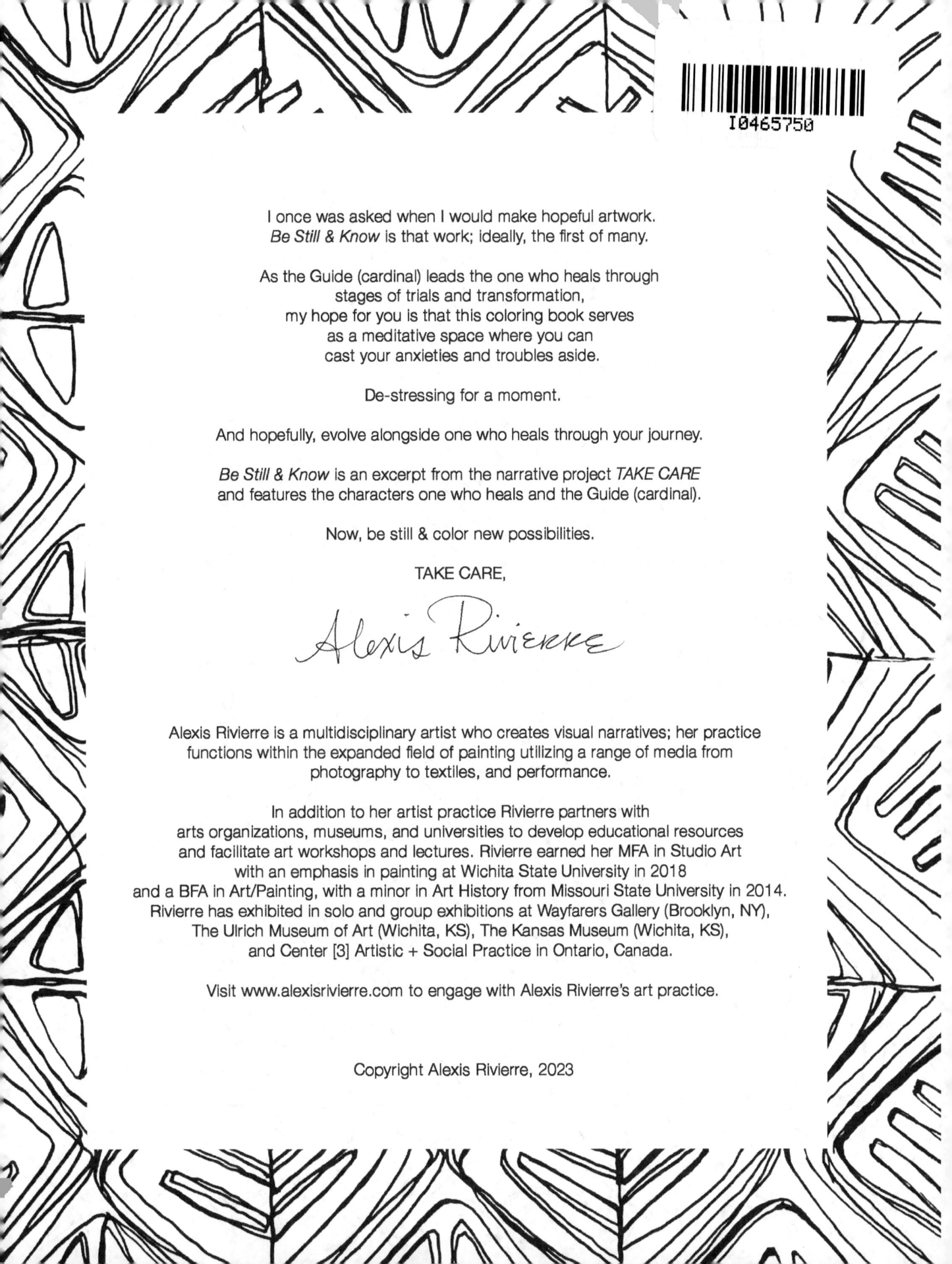

I once was asked when I would make hopeful artwork.
Be Still & Know is that work; ideally, the first of many.

As the Guide (cardinal) leads the one who heals through
stages of trials and transformation,
my hope for you is that this coloring book serves
as a meditative space where you can
cast your anxieties and troubles aside.

De-stressing for a moment.

And hopefully, evolve alongside one who heals through your journey.

Be Still & Know is an excerpt from the narrative project *TAKE CARE*
and features the characters one who heals and the Guide (cardinal).

Now, be still & color new possibilities.

TAKE CARE,

Alexis Rivierre

Alexis Rivierre is a multidisciplinary artist who creates visual narratives; her practice
functions within the expanded field of painting utilizing a range of media from
photography to textiles, and performance.

In addition to her artist practice Rivierre partners with
arts organizations, museums, and universities to develop educational resources
and facilitate art workshops and lectures. Rivierre earned her MFA in Studio Art
with an emphasis in painting at Wichita State University in 2018
and a BFA in Art/Painting, with a minor in Art History from Missouri State University in 2014.
Rivierre has exhibited in solo and group exhibitions at Wayfarers Gallery (Brooklyn, NY),
The Ulrich Museum of Art (Wichita, KS), The Kansas Museum (Wichita, KS),
and Center [3] Artistic + Social Practice in Ontario, Canada.

Visit www.alexisrivierre.com to engage with Alexis Rivierre's art practice.

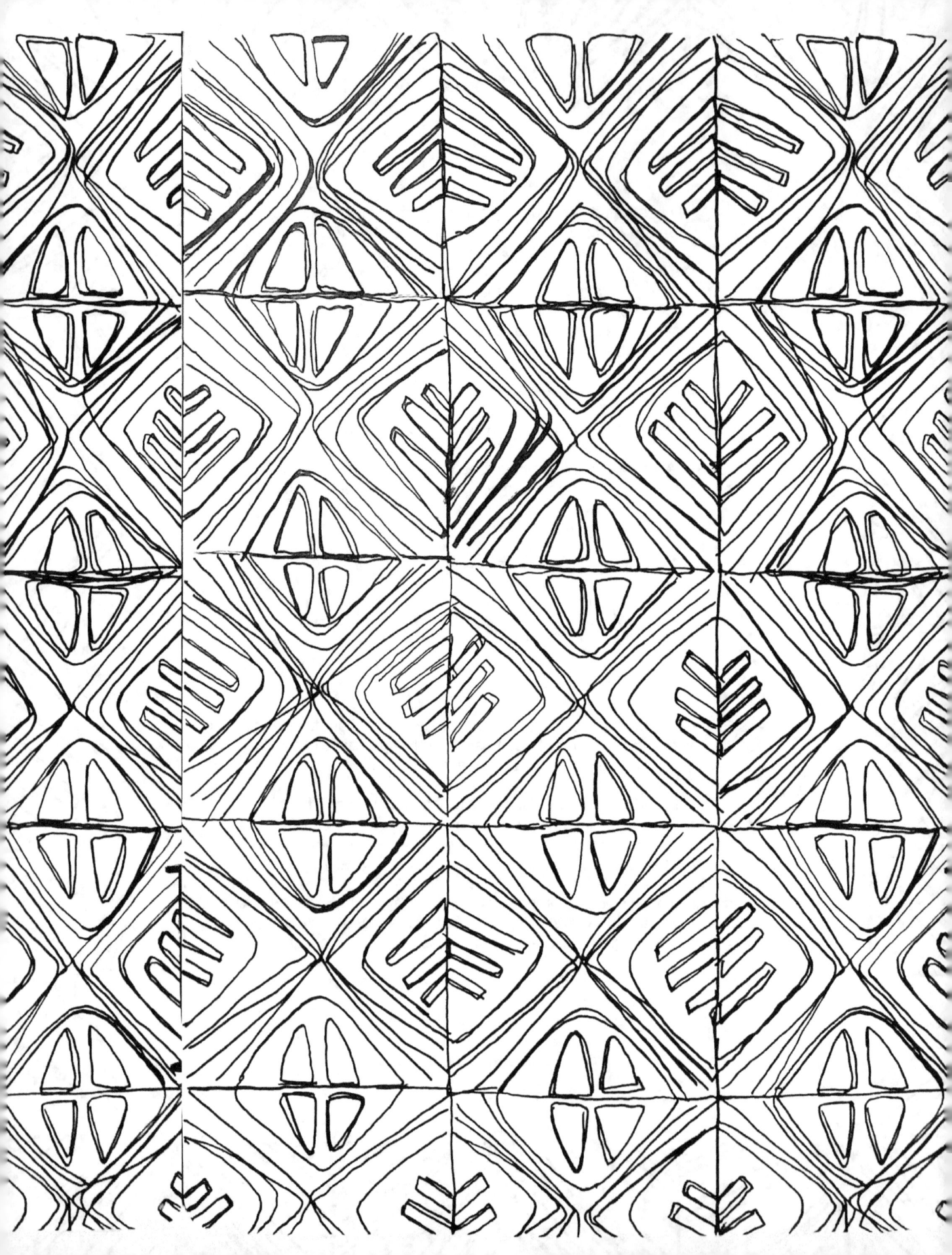

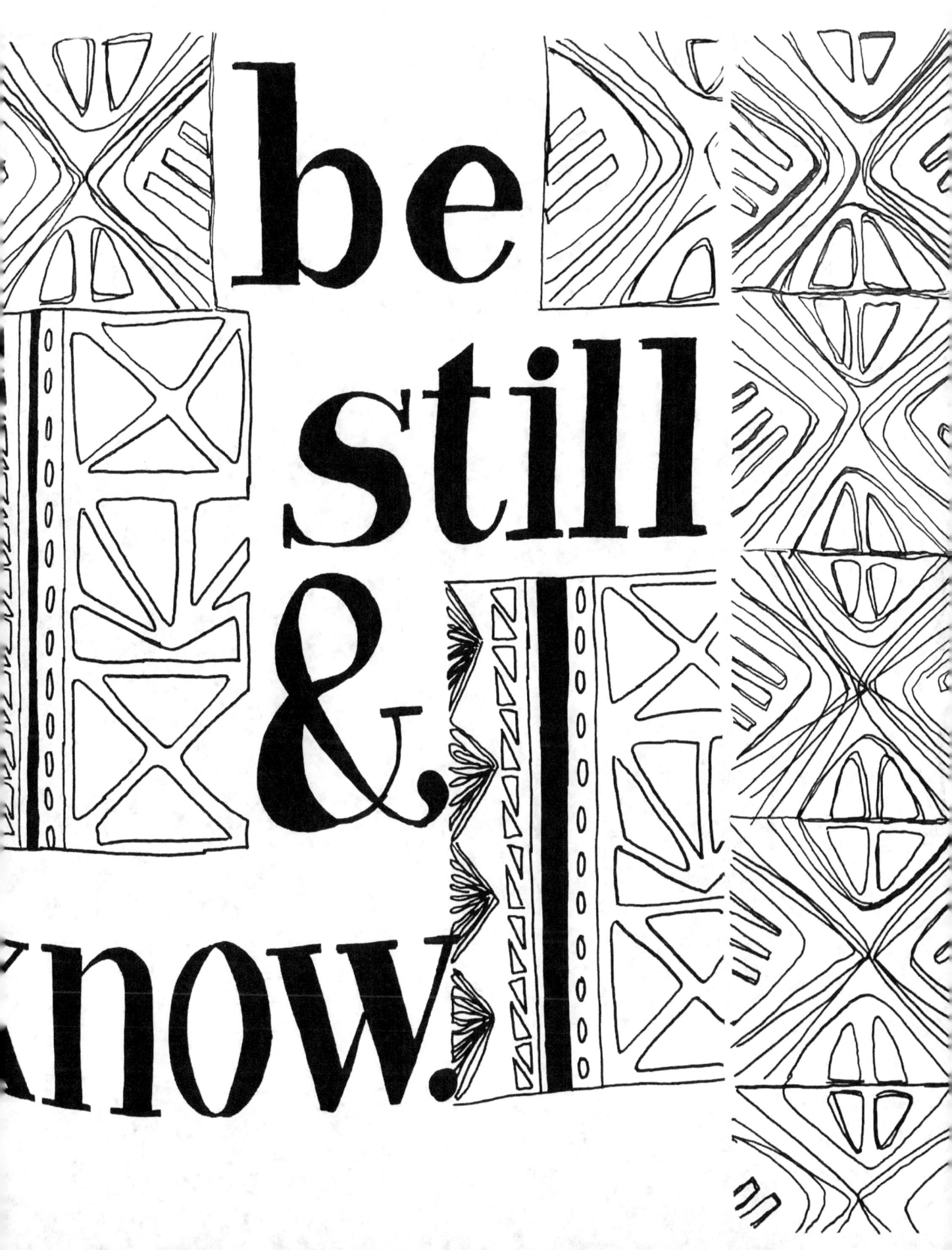

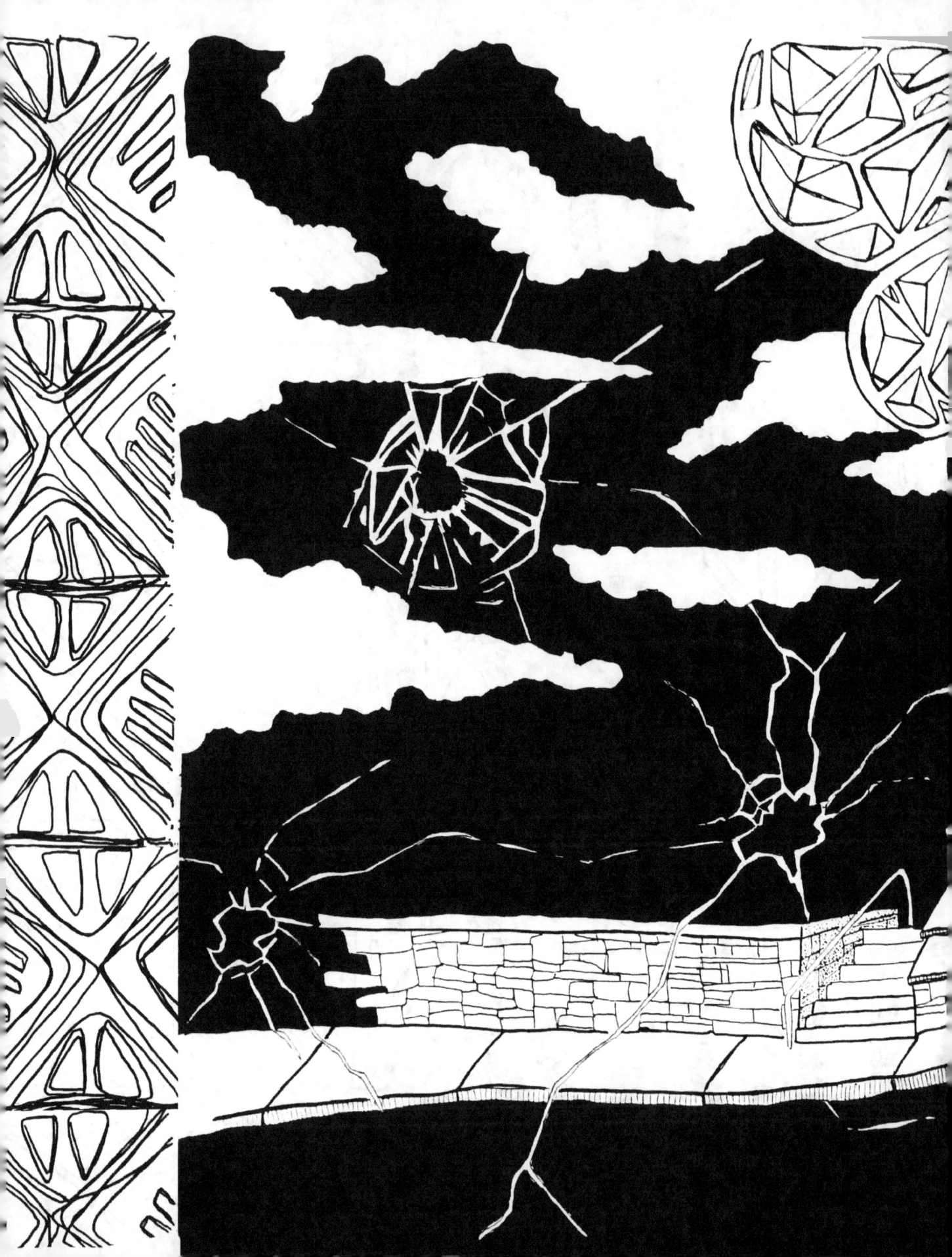

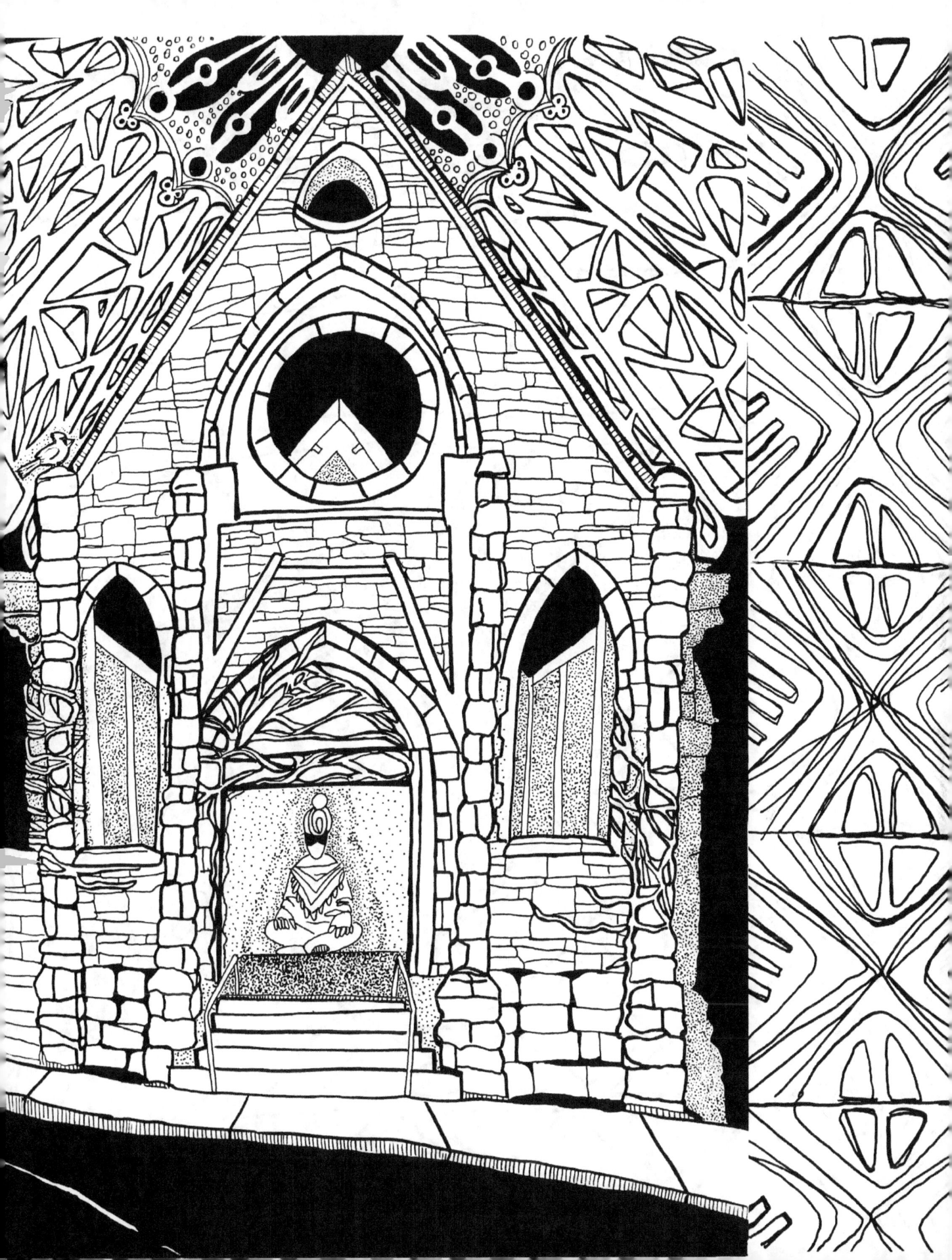

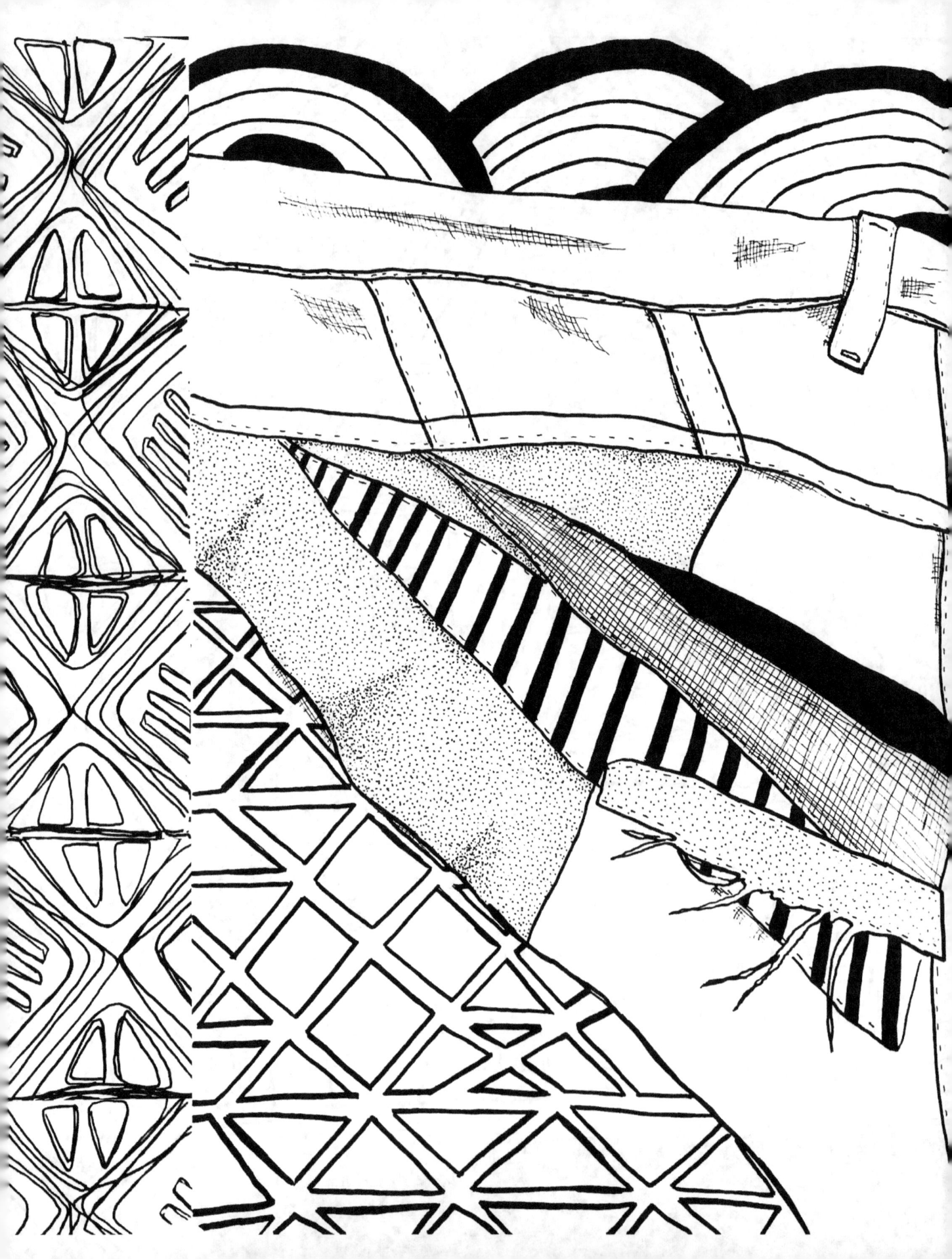

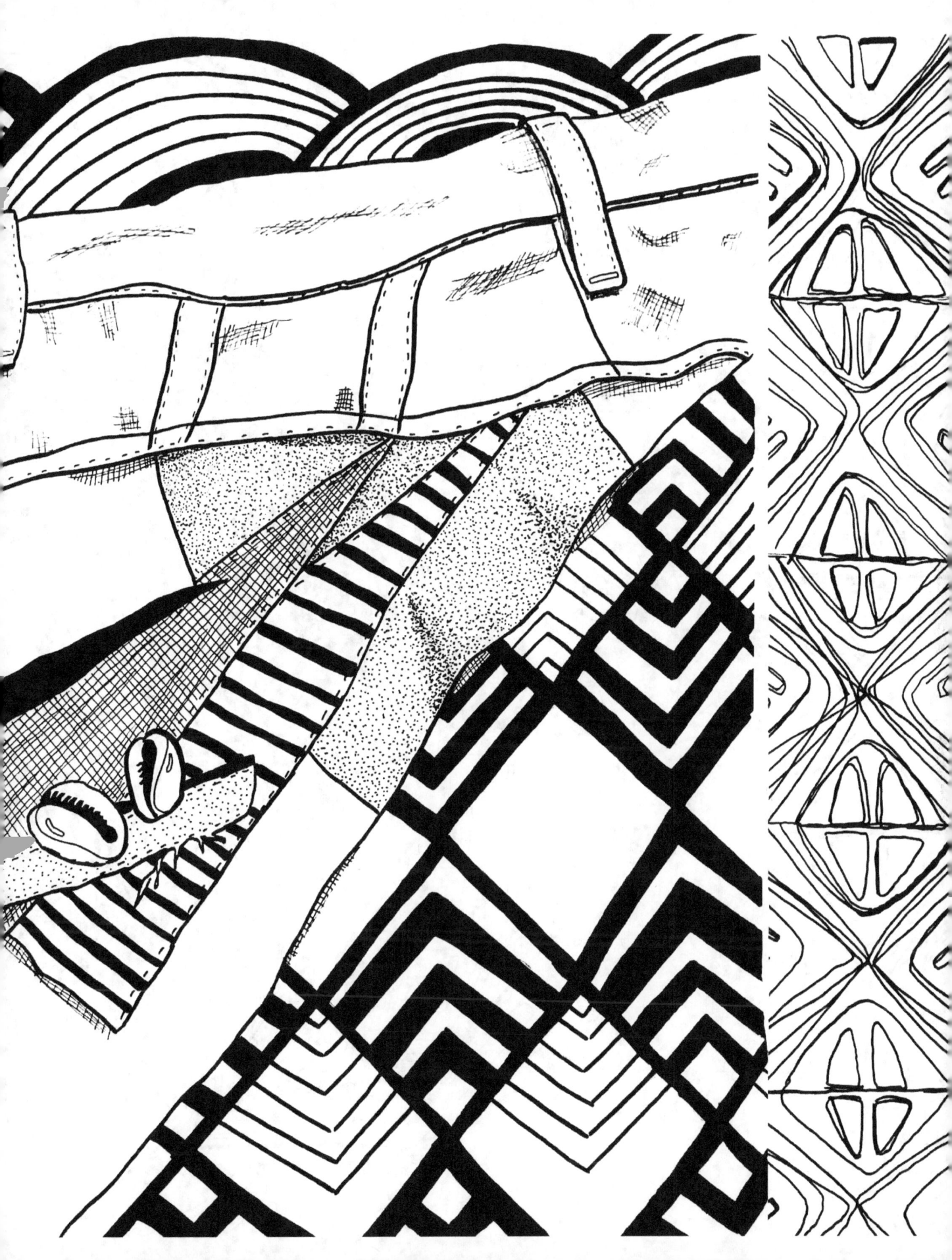

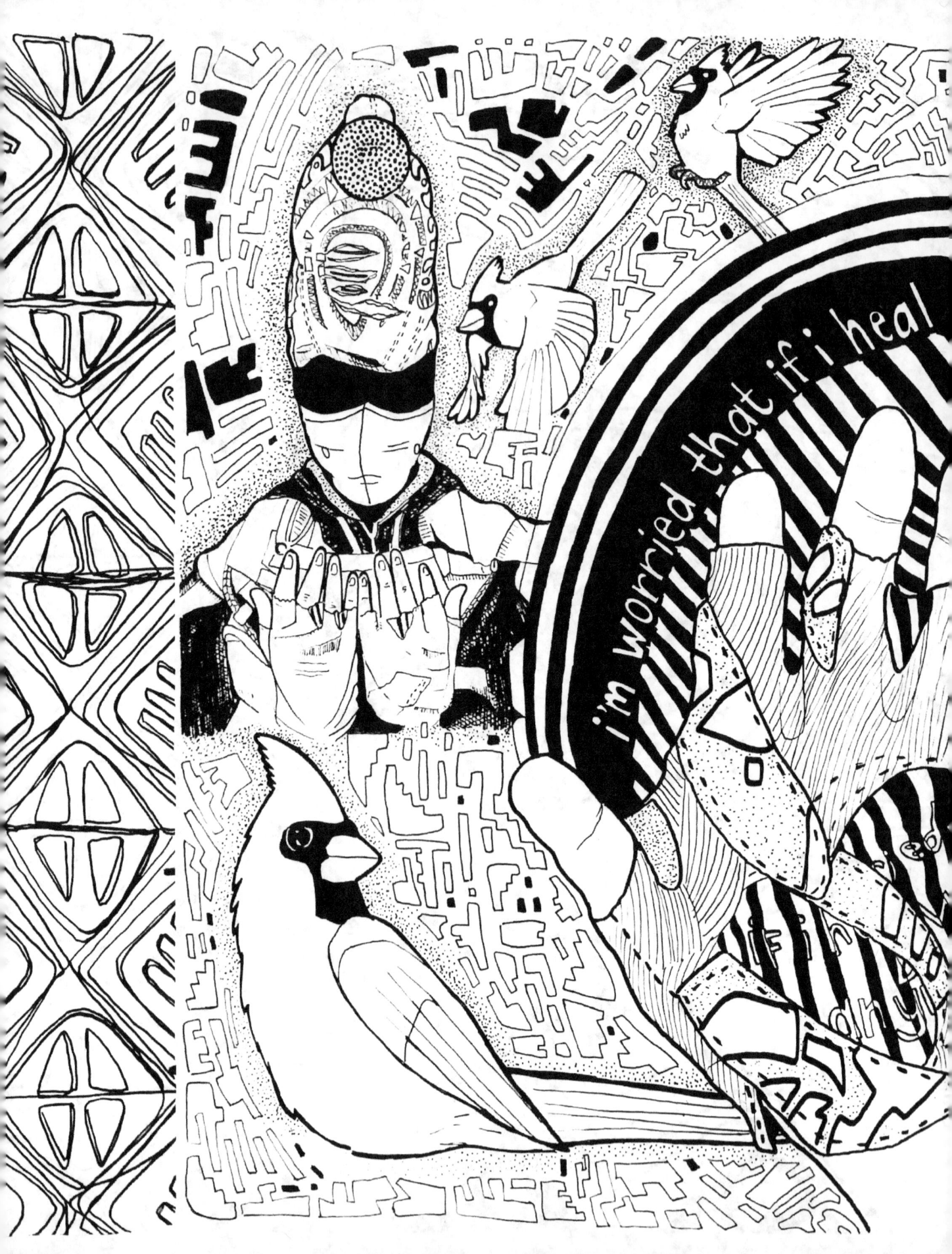

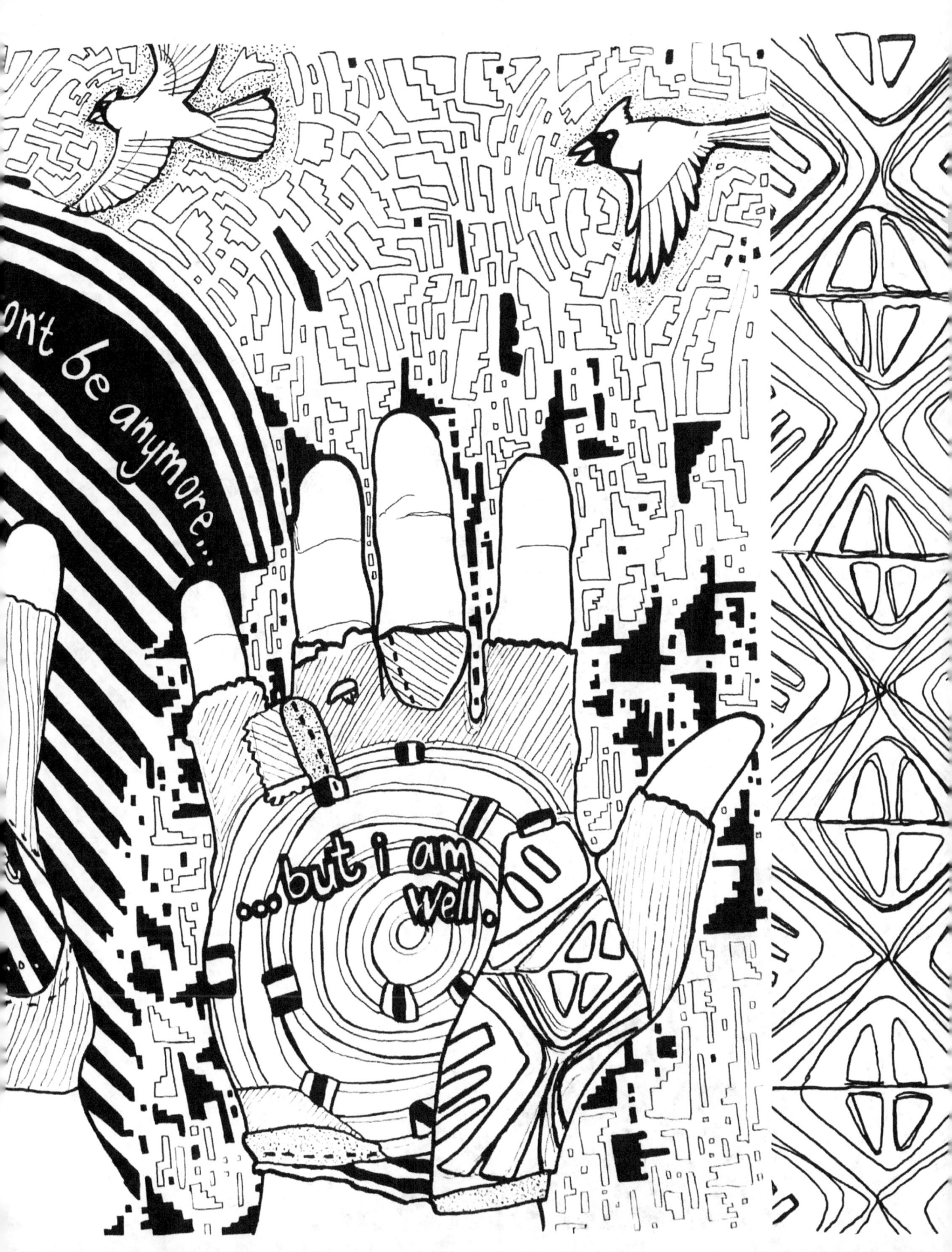

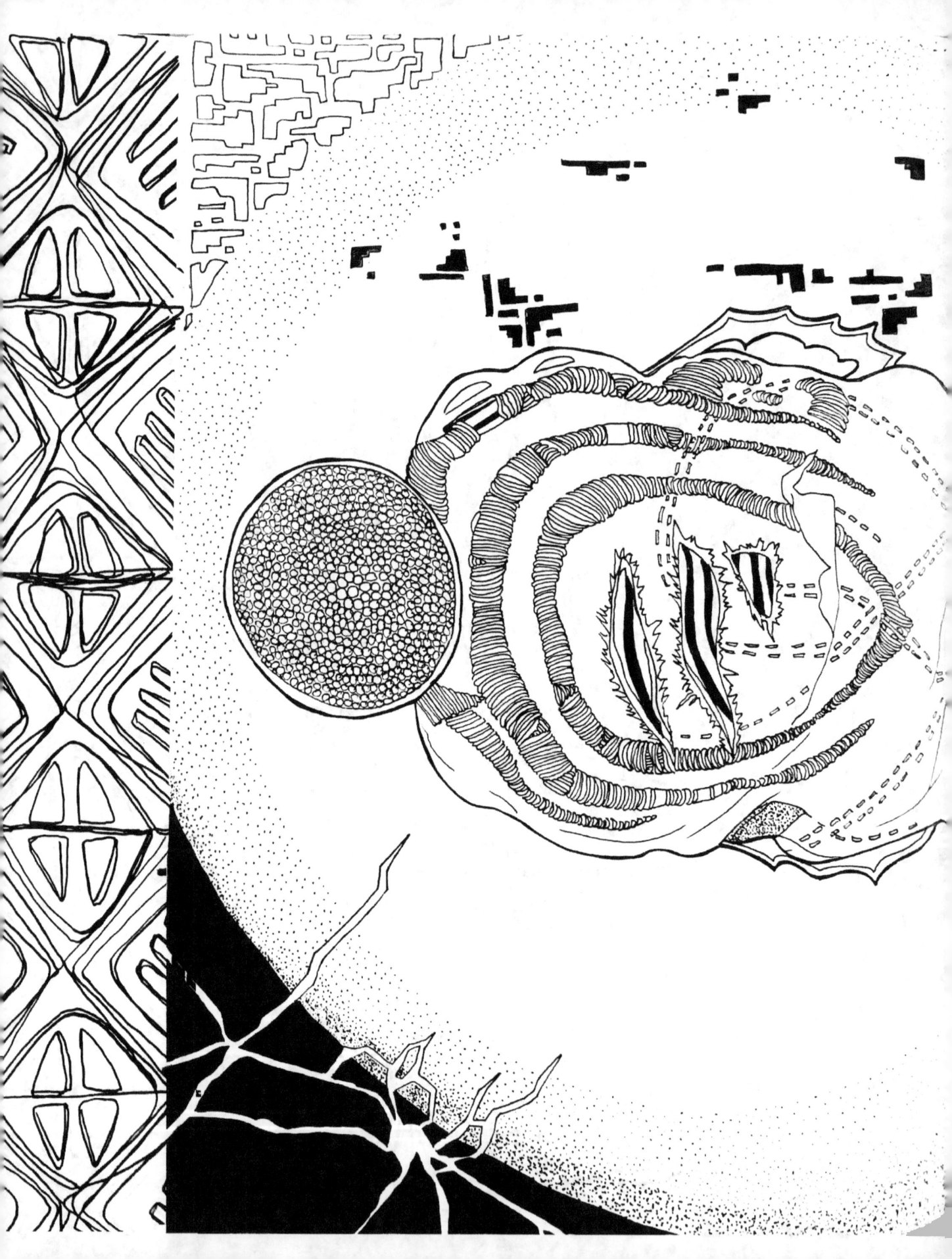

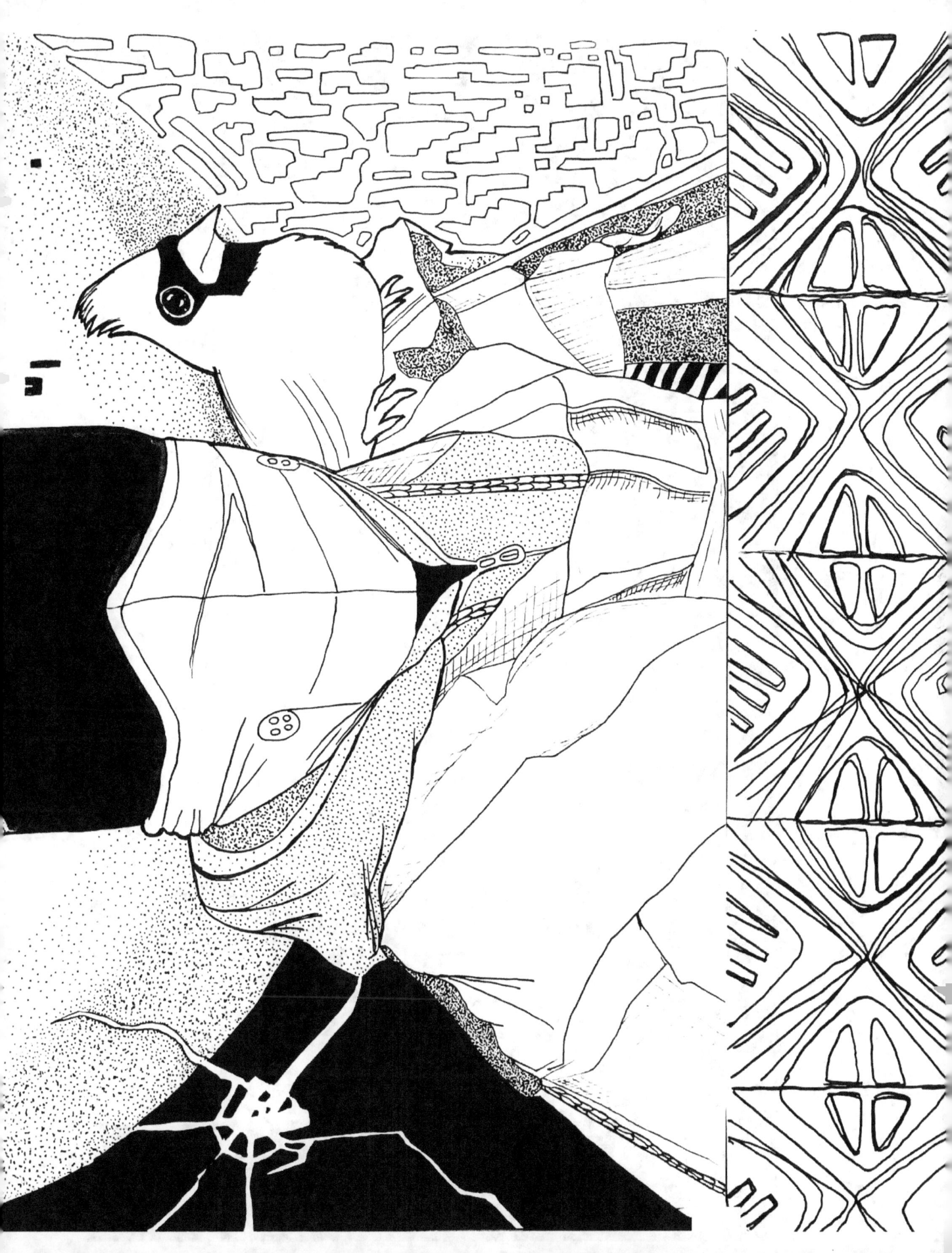

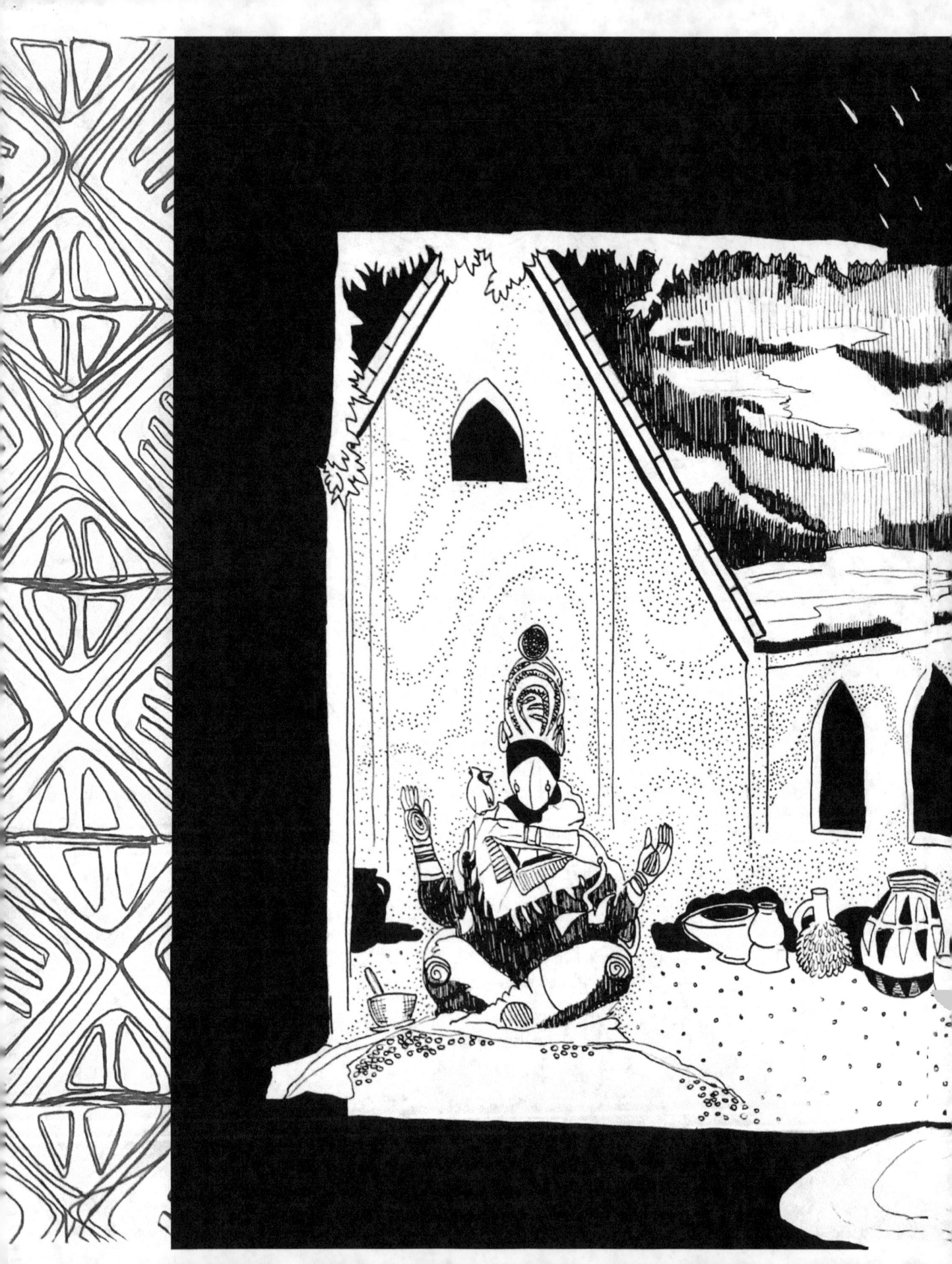

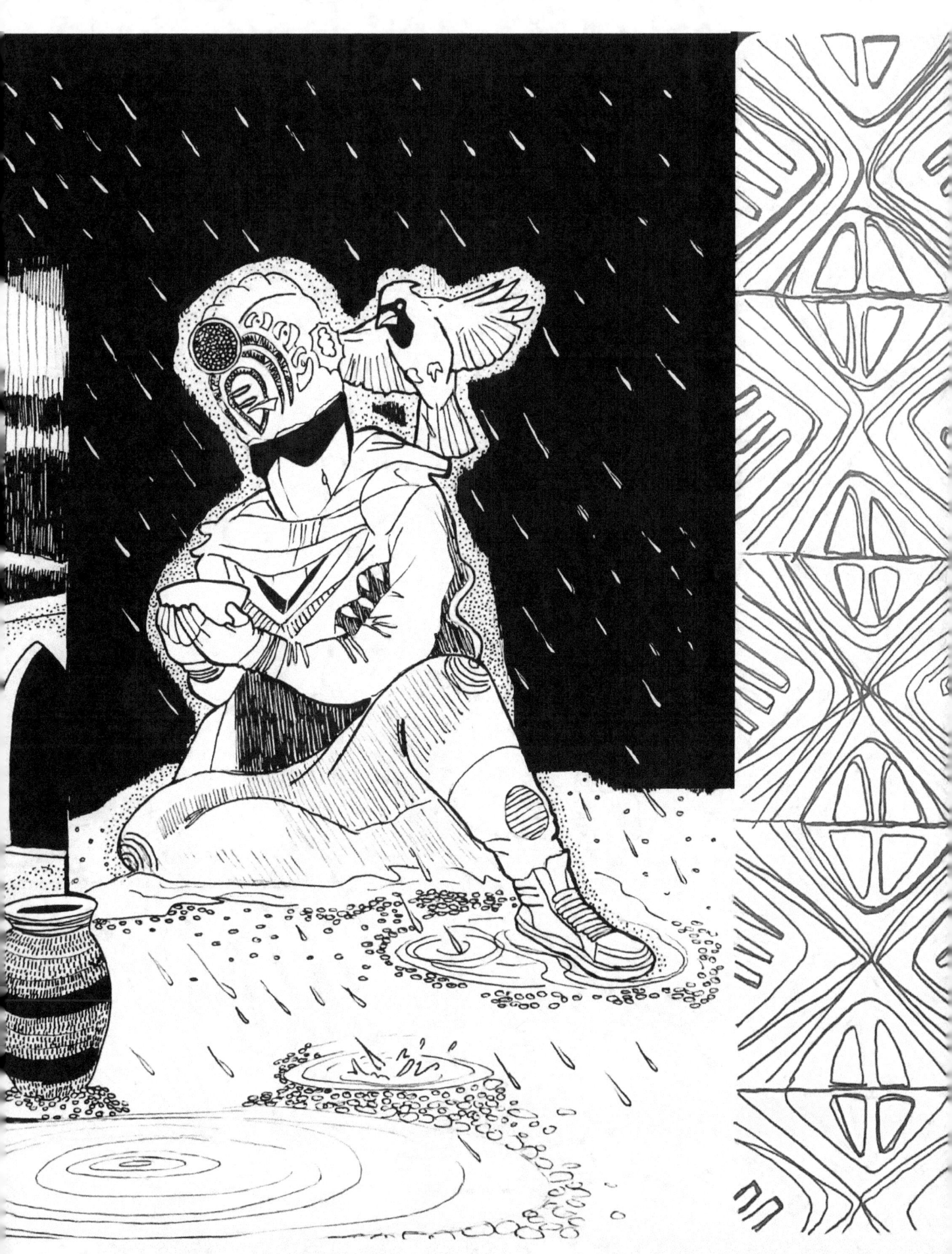

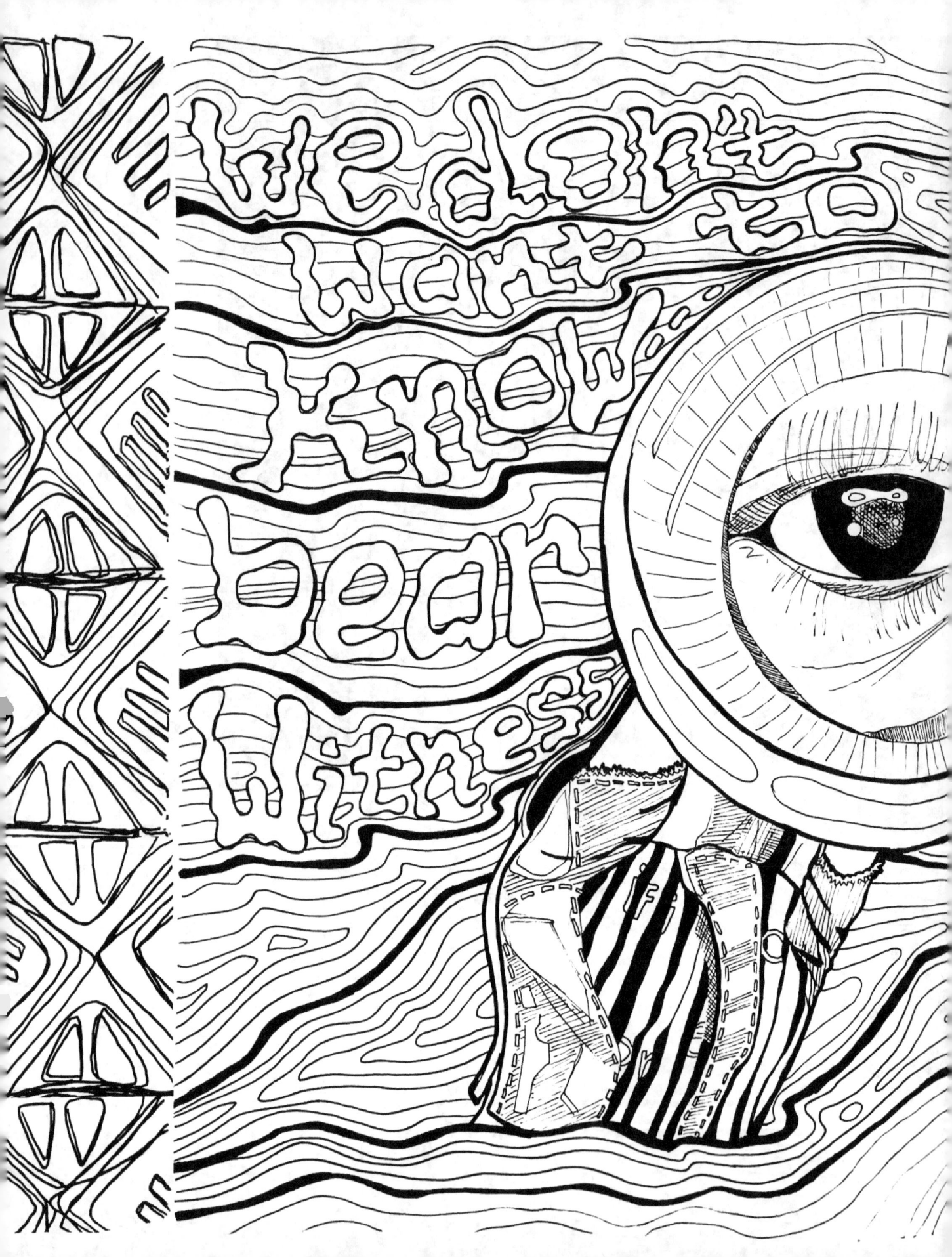

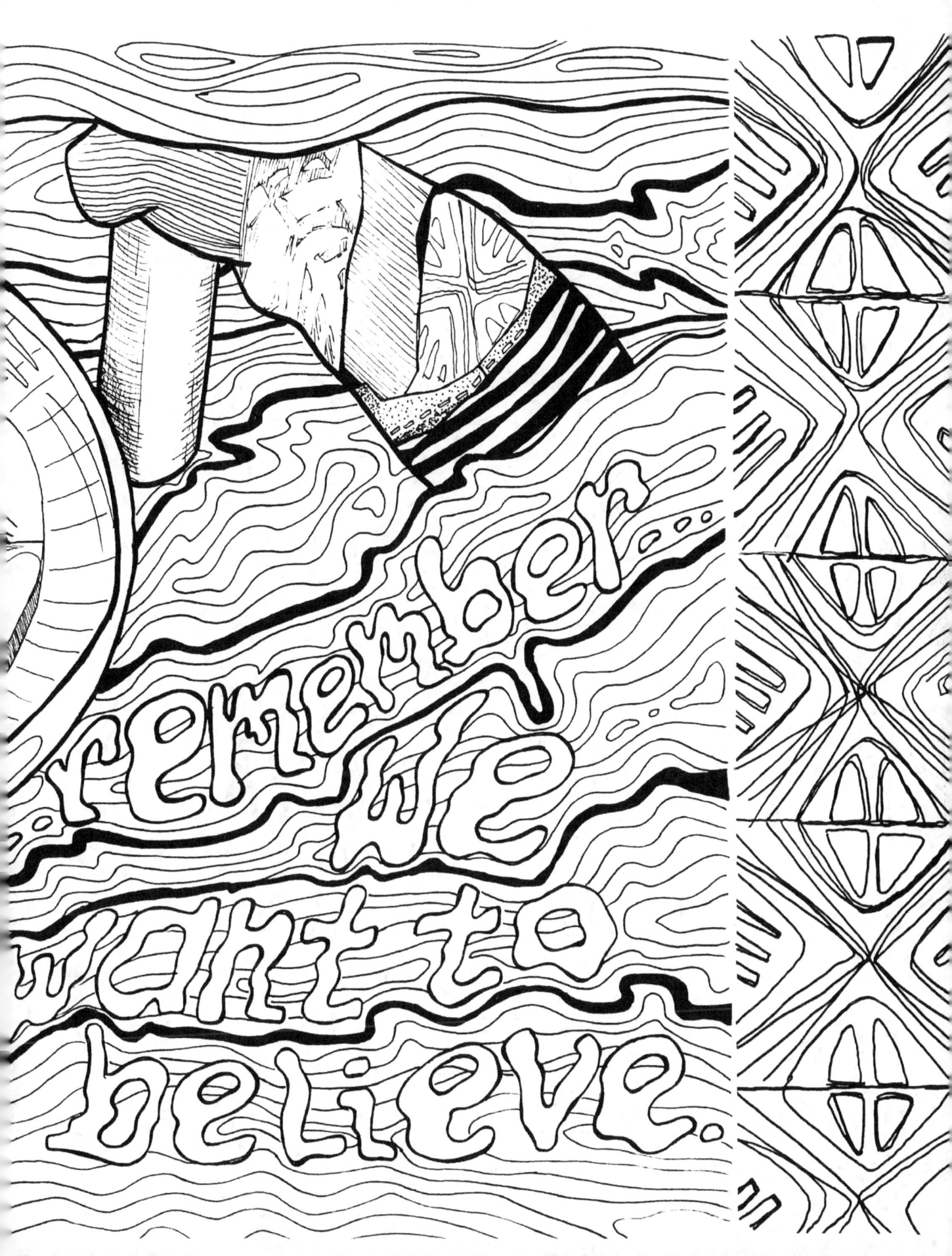

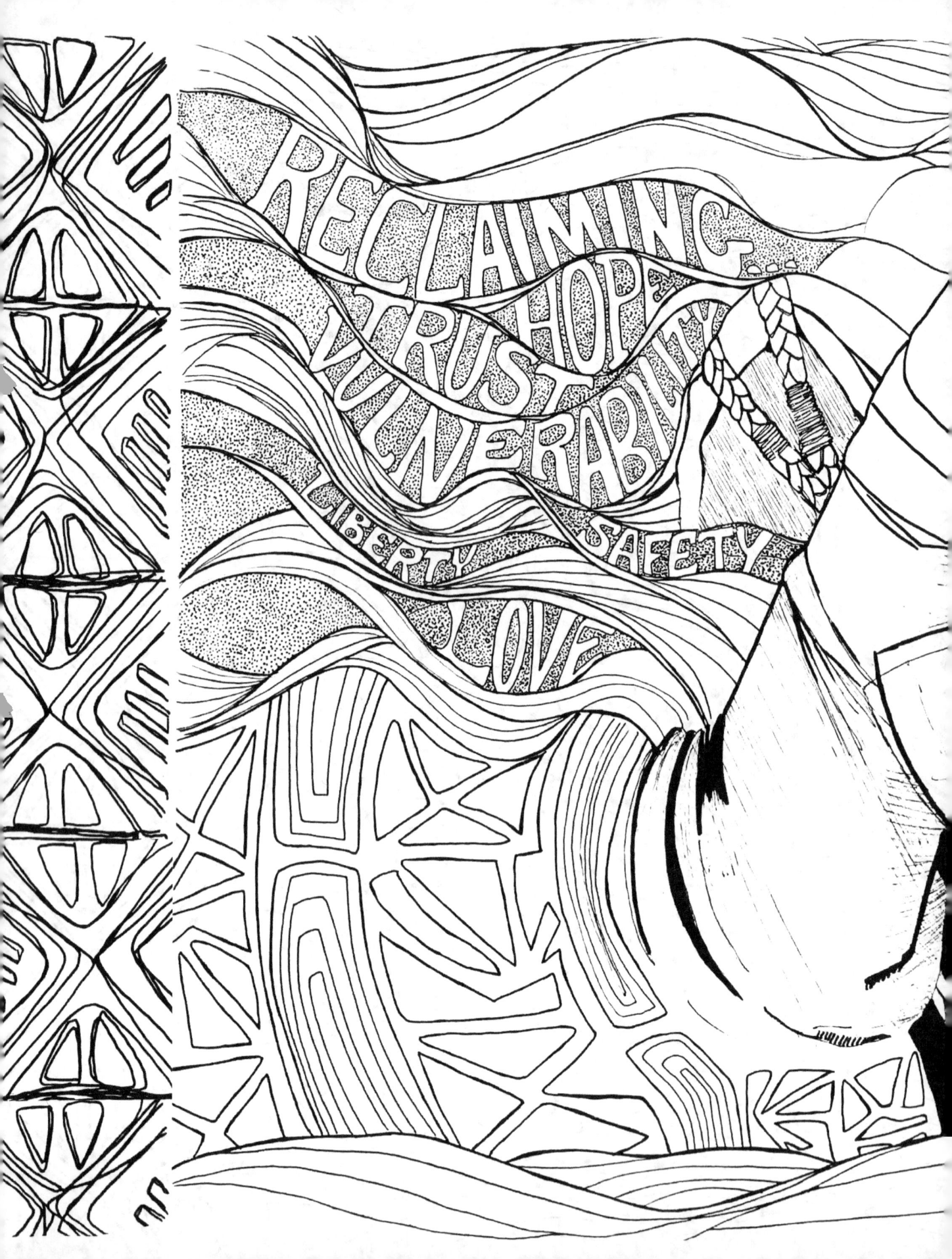

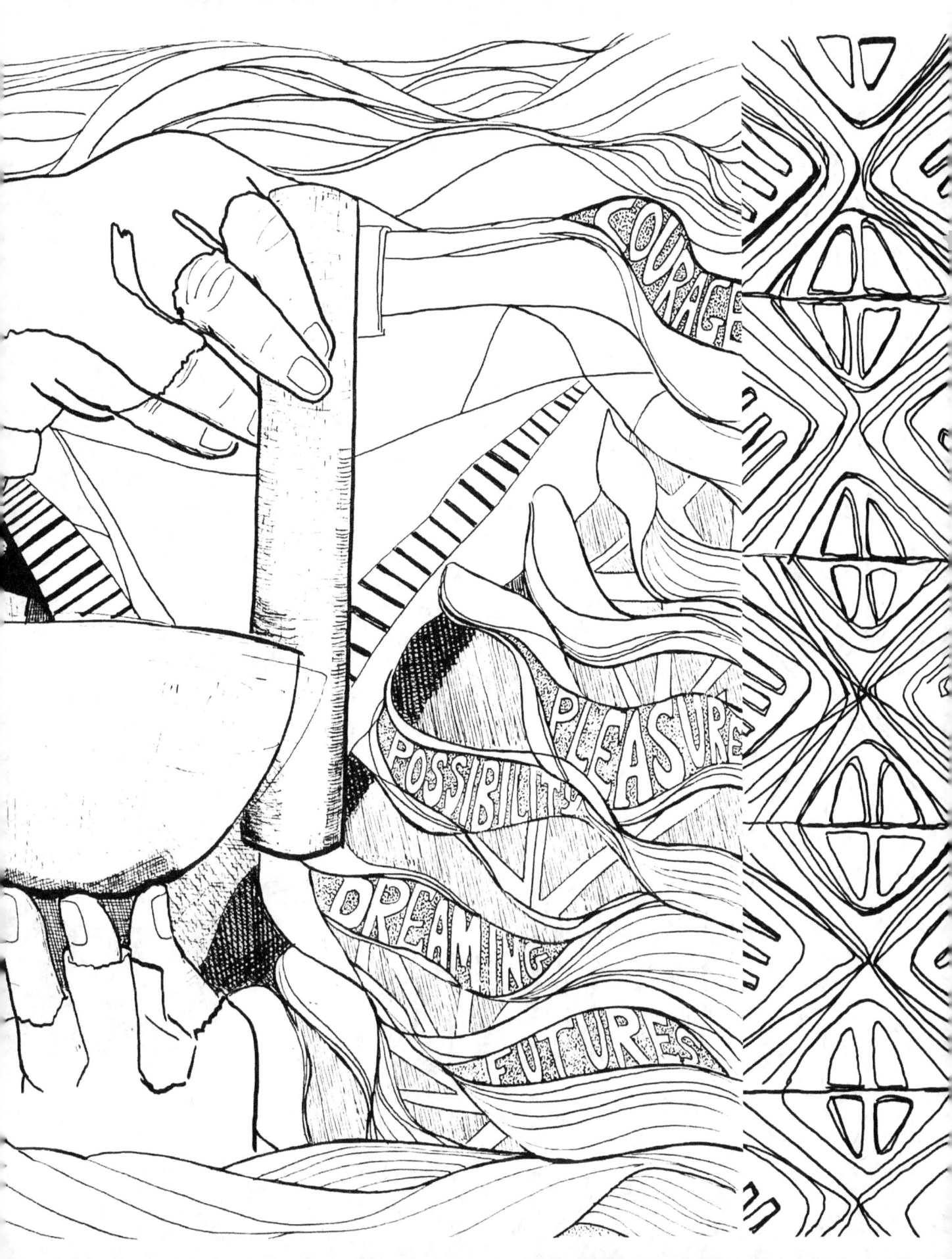

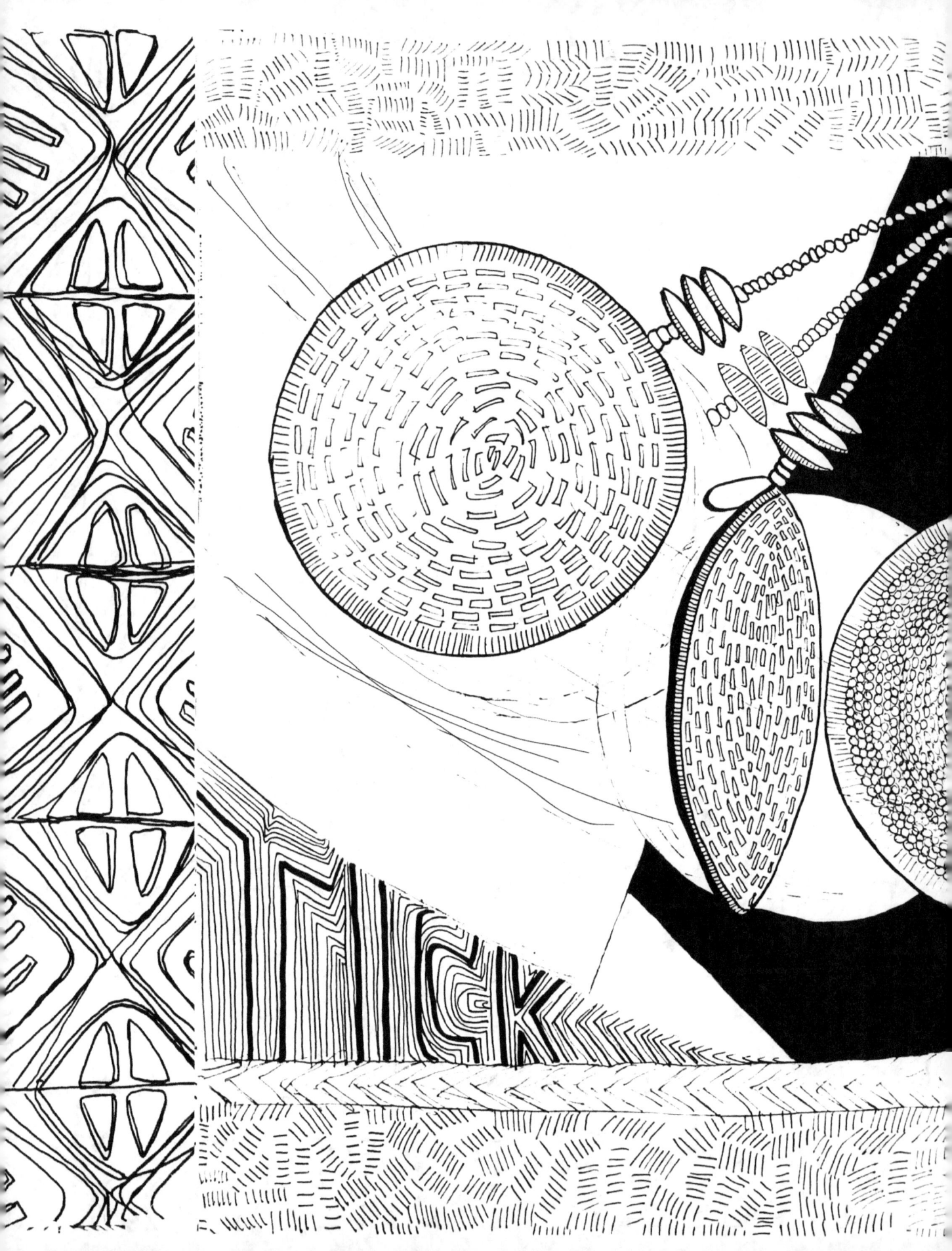

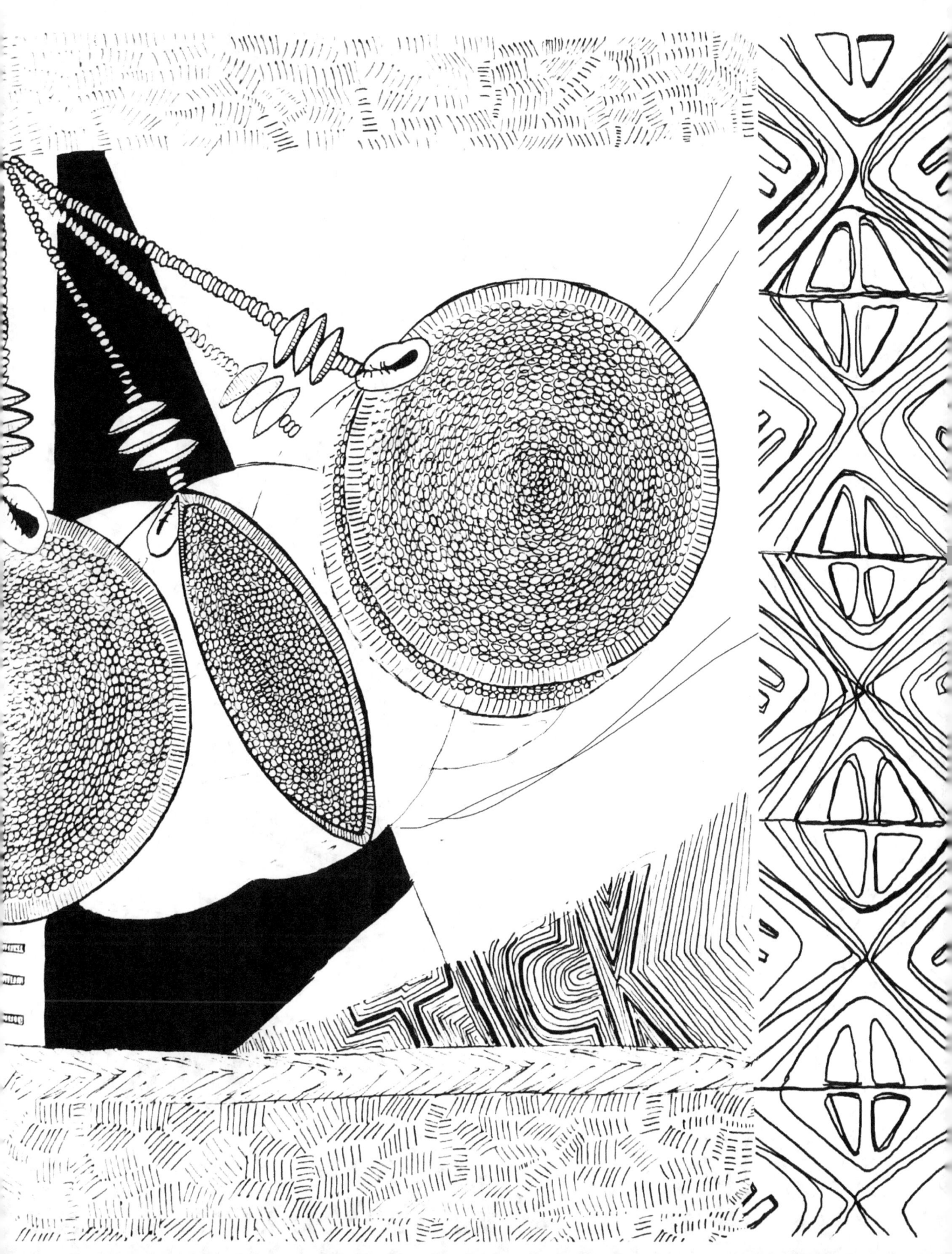

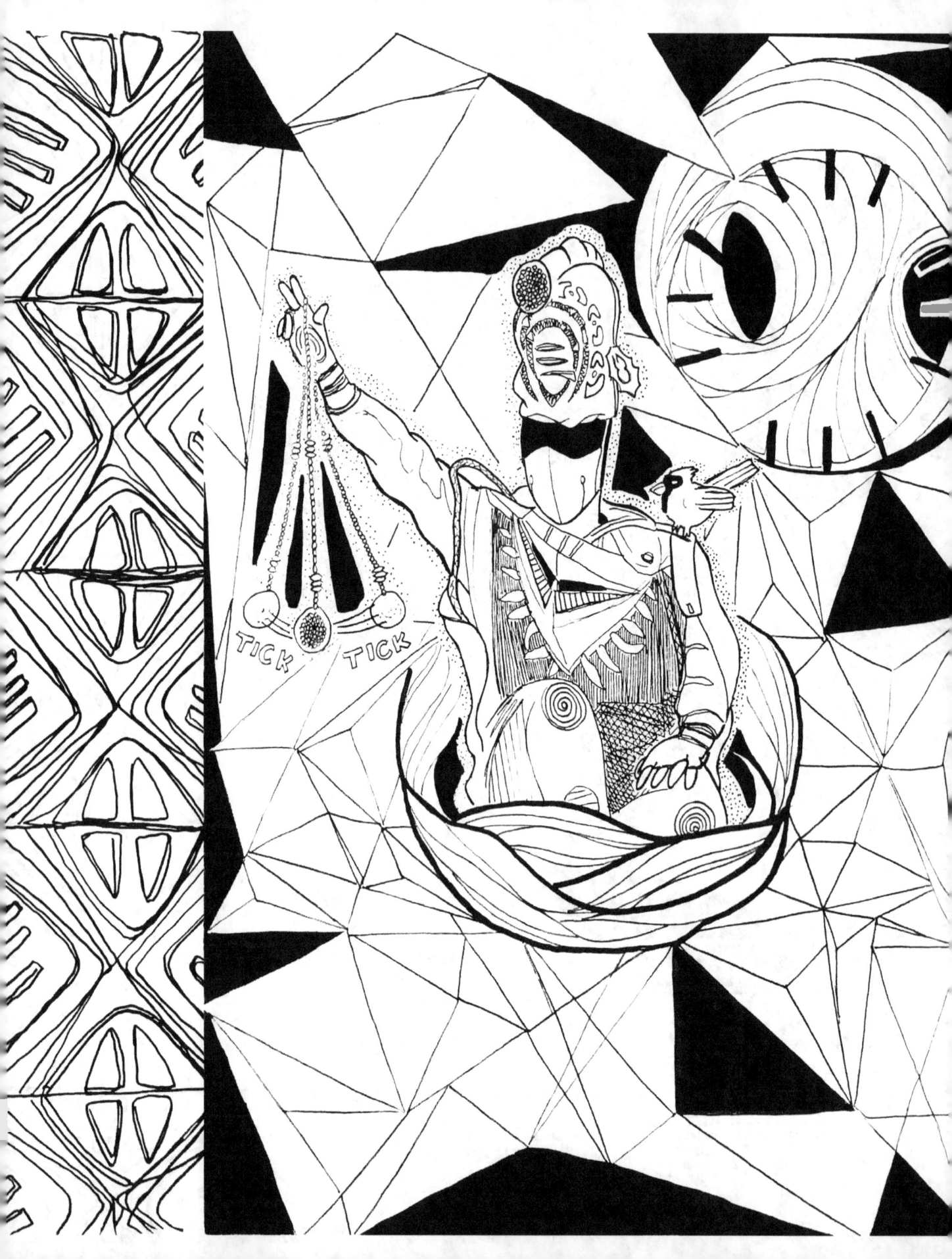

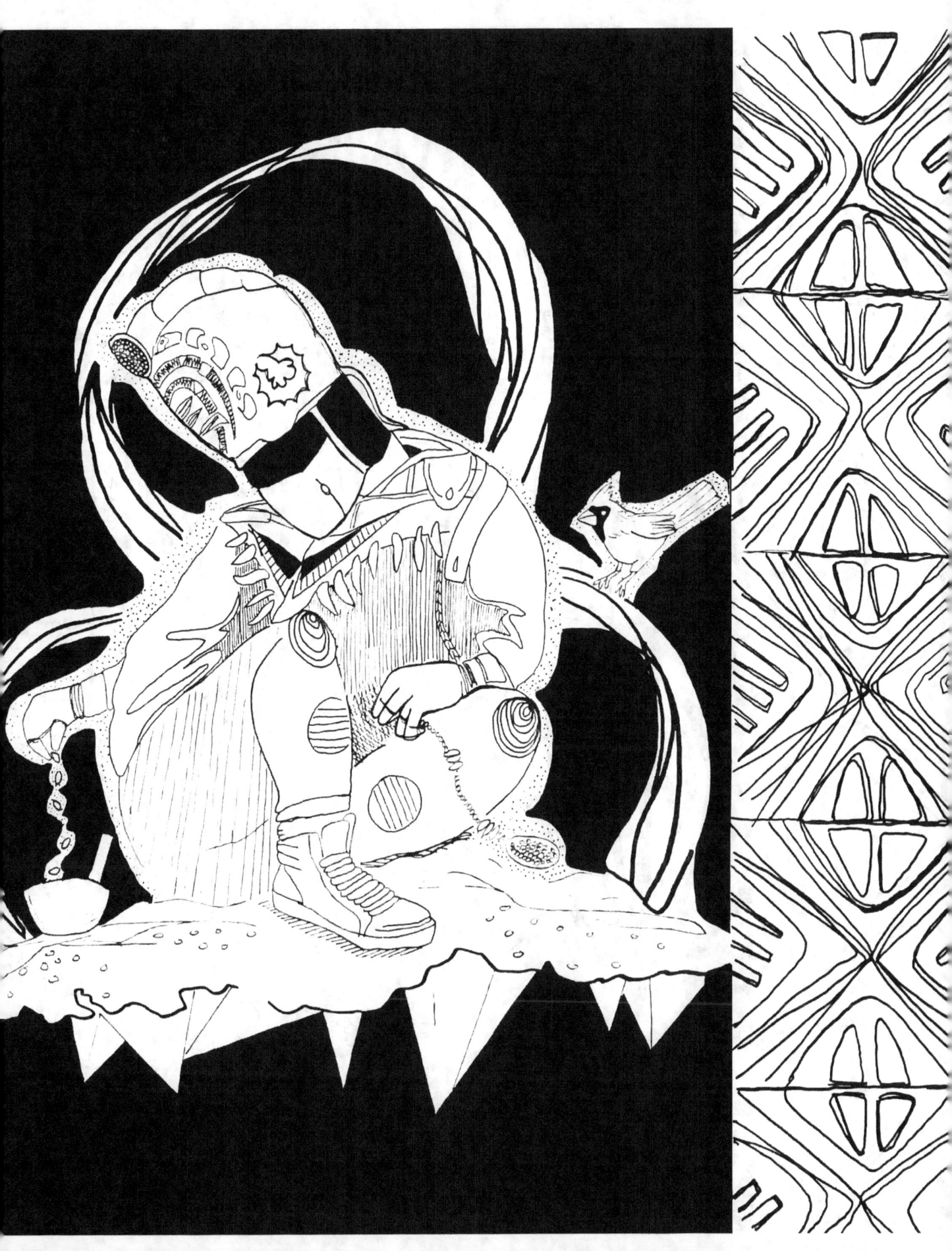

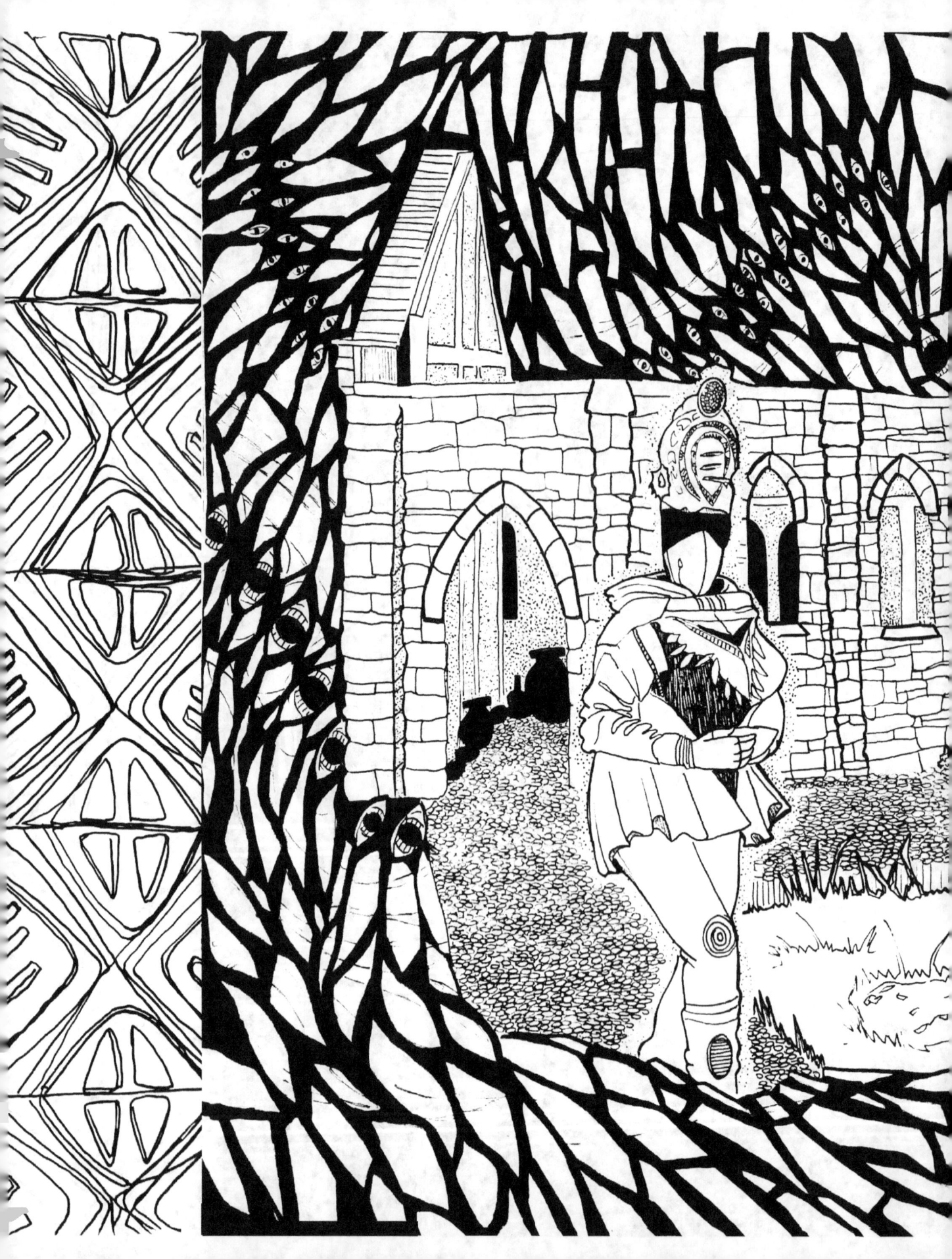

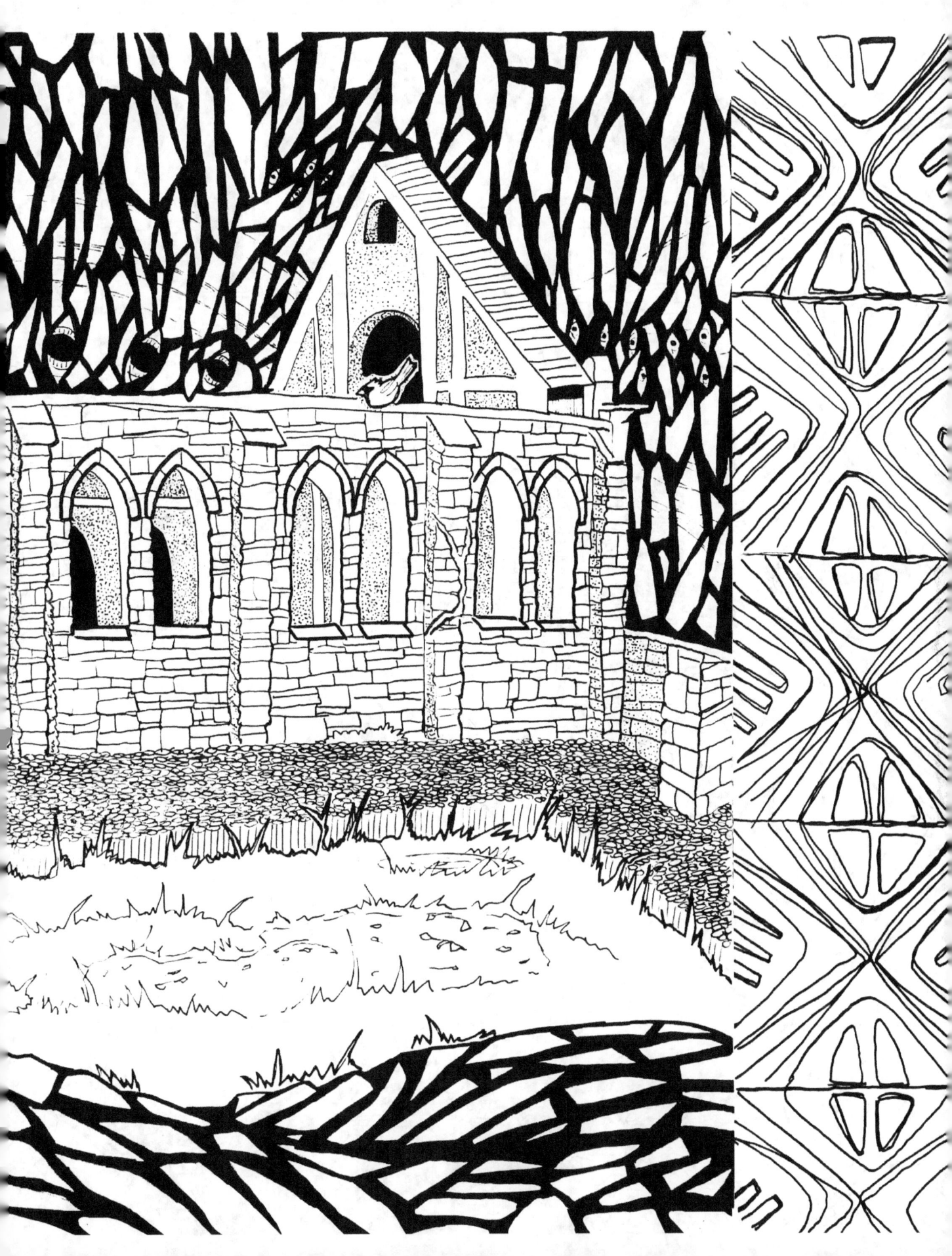

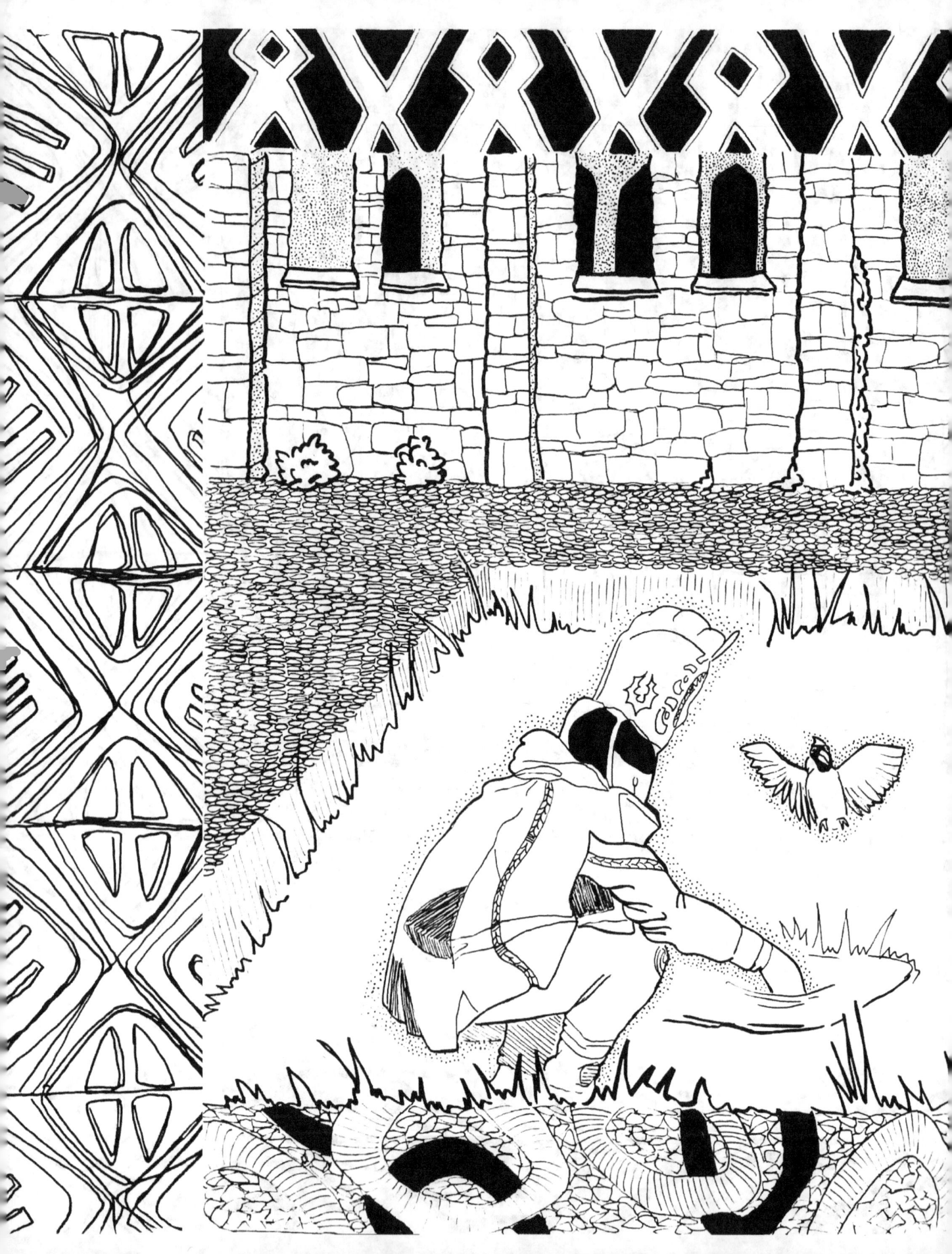

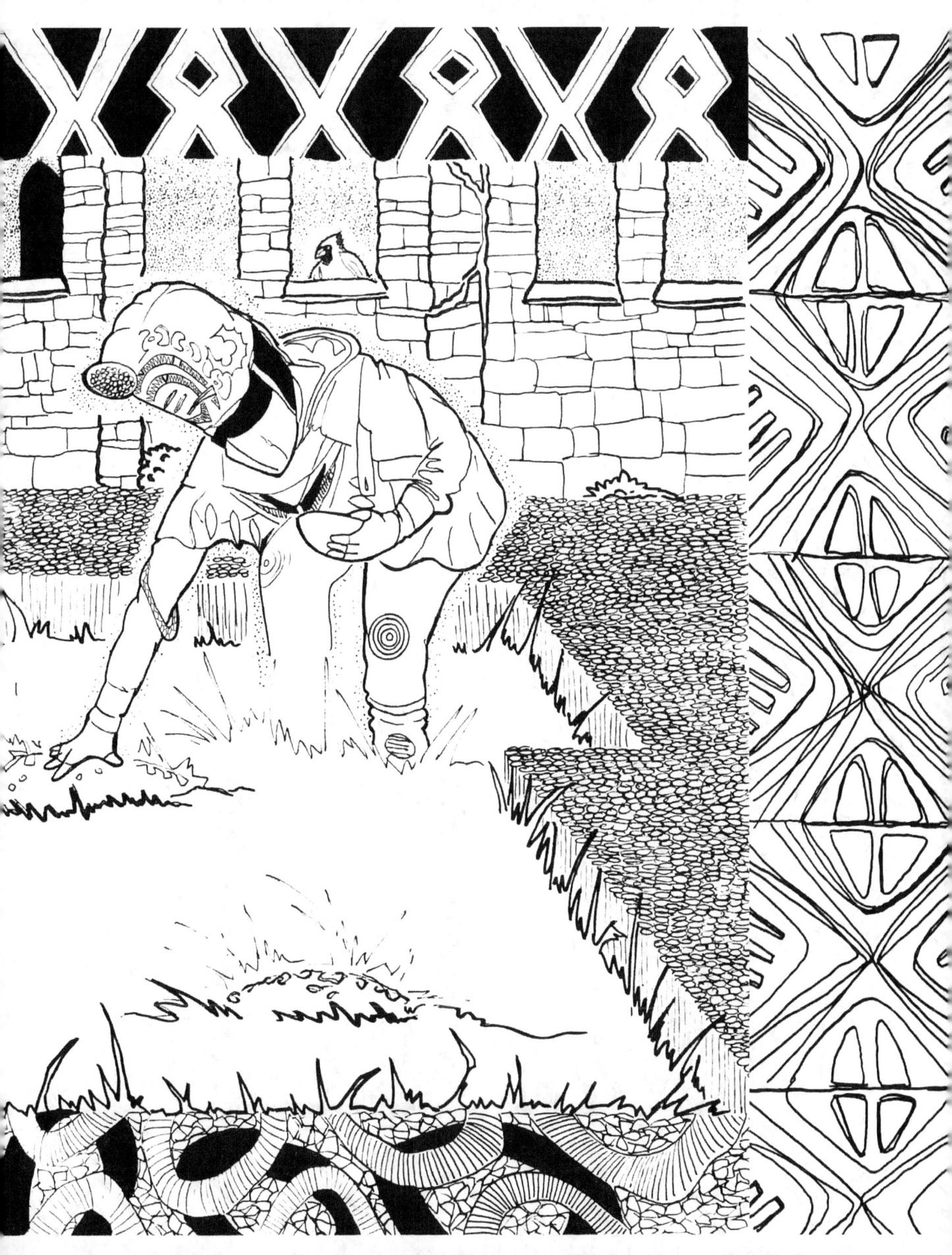

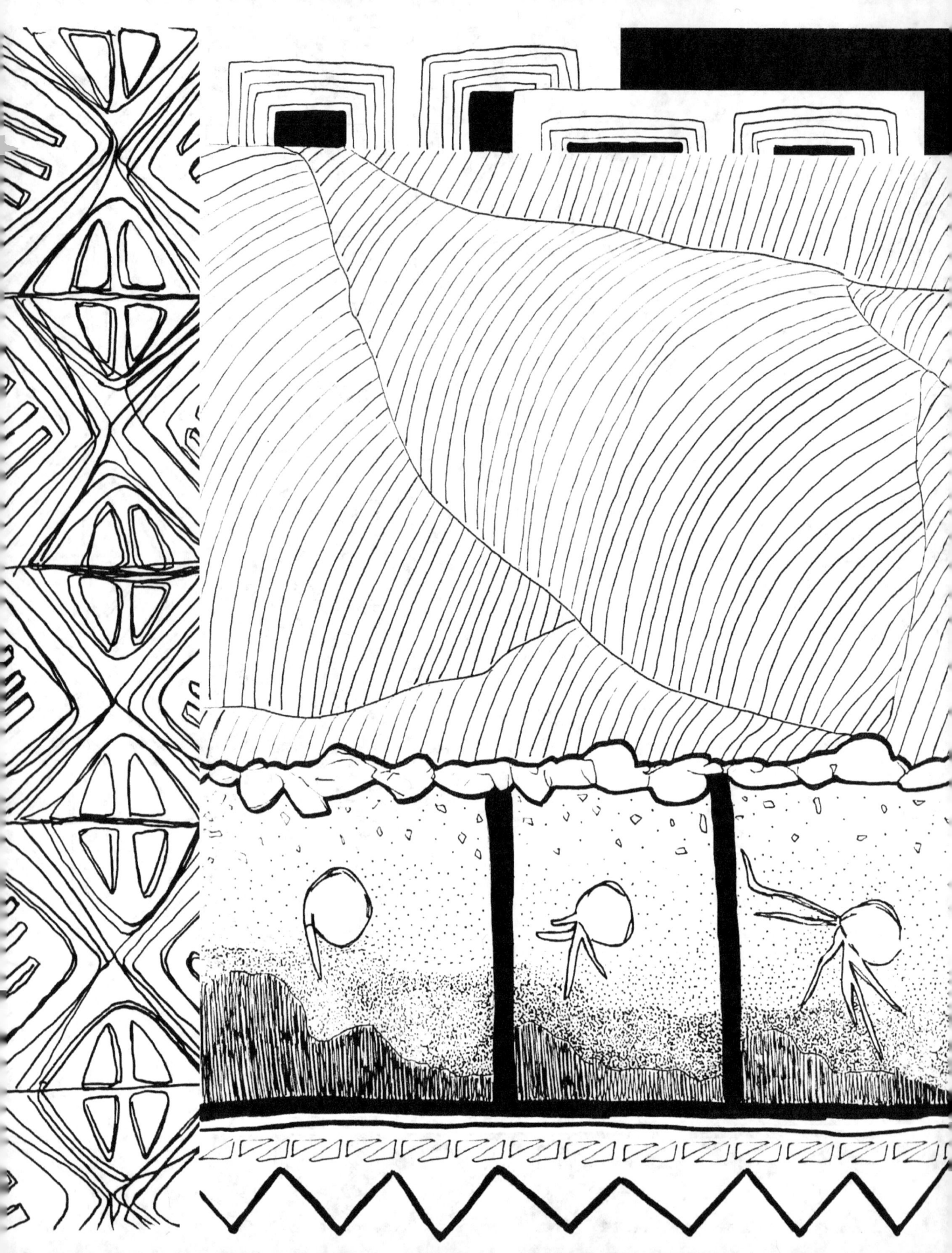

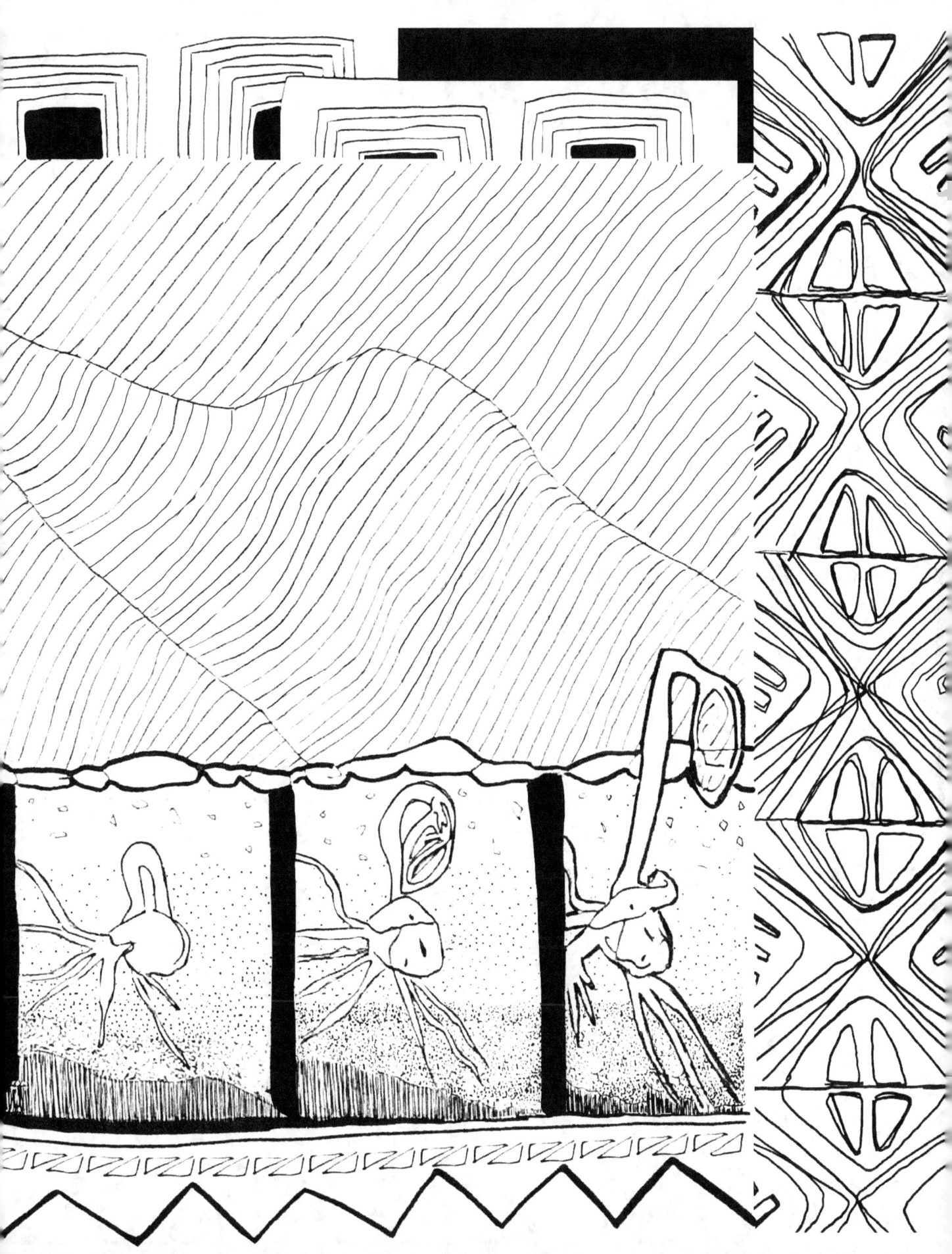

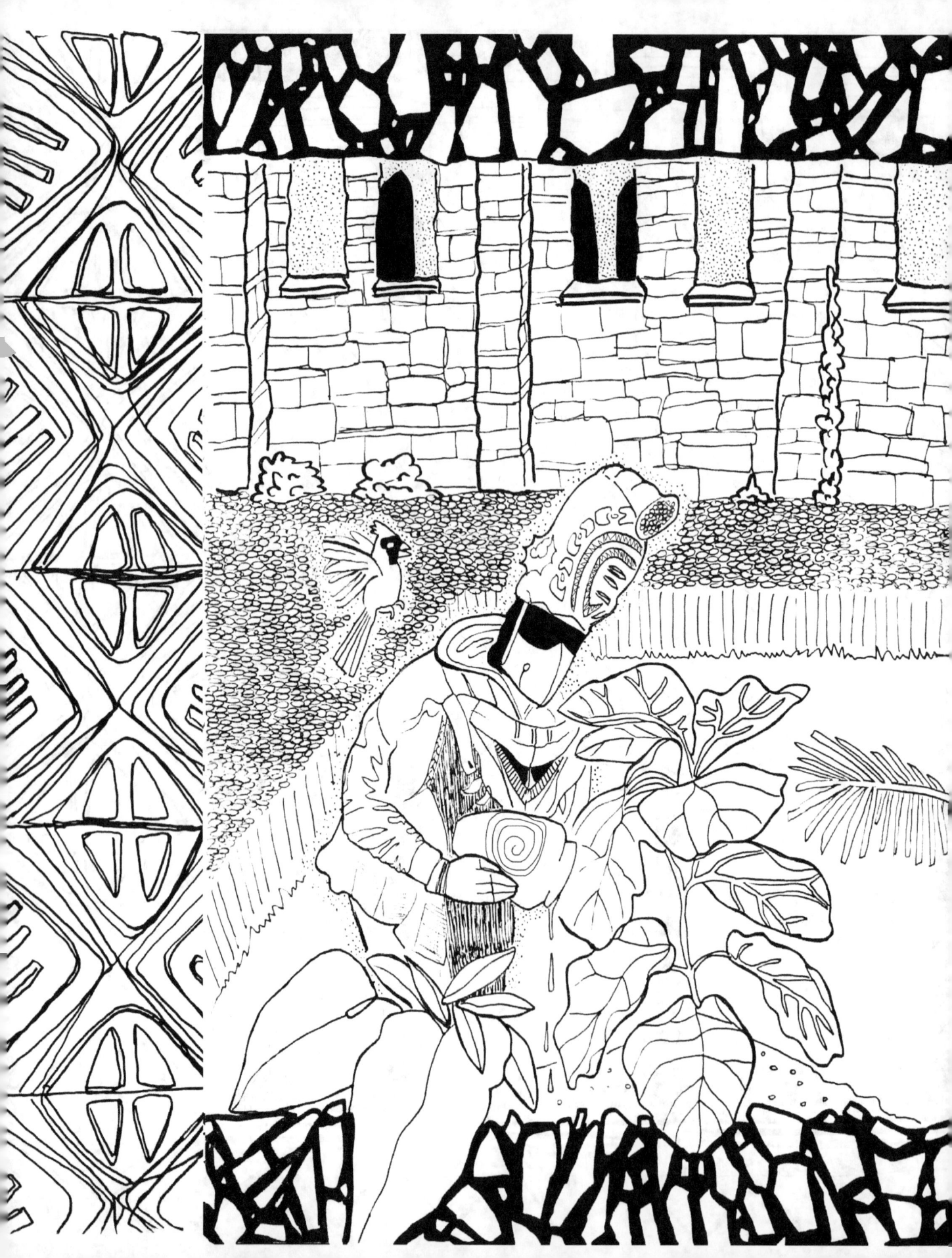

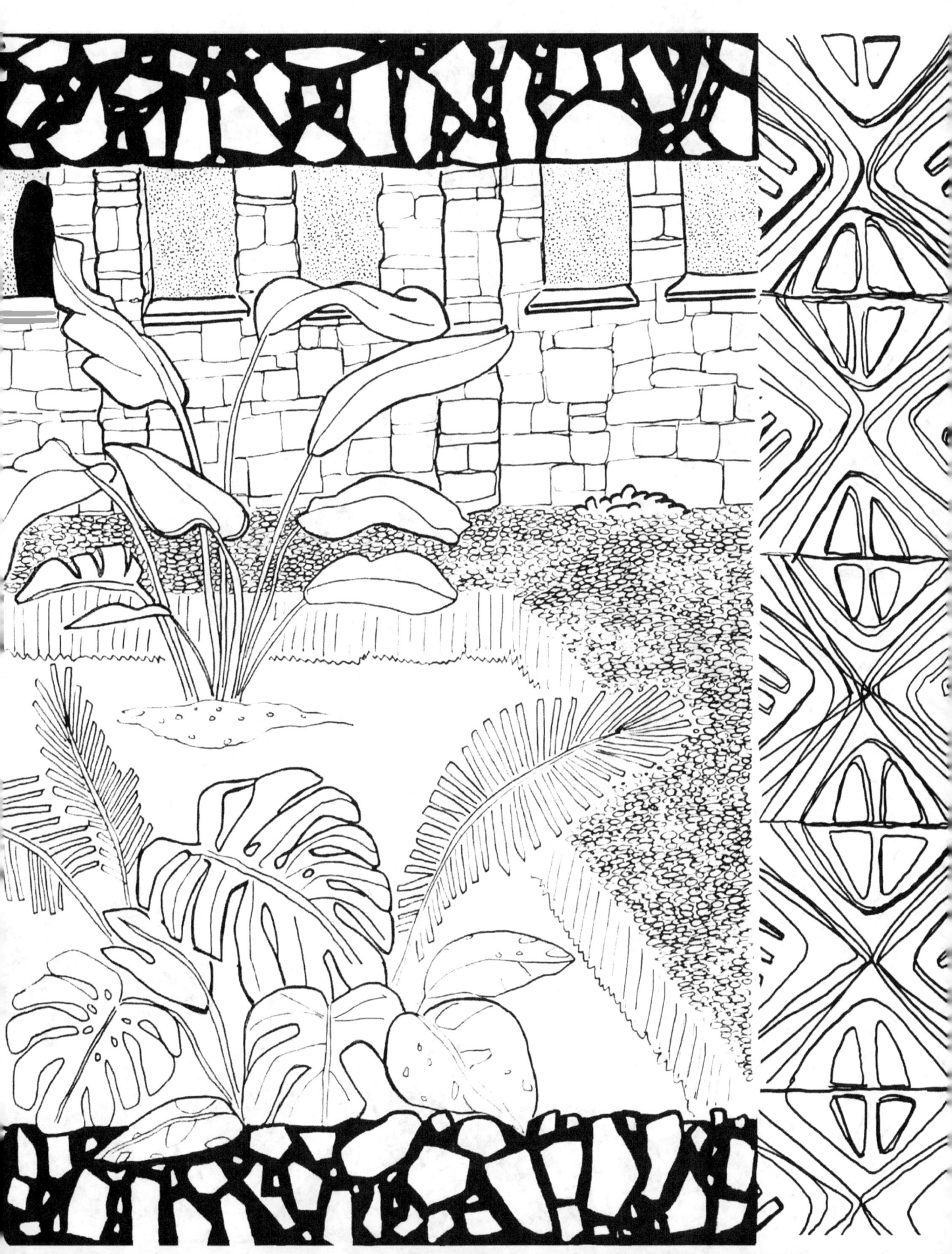

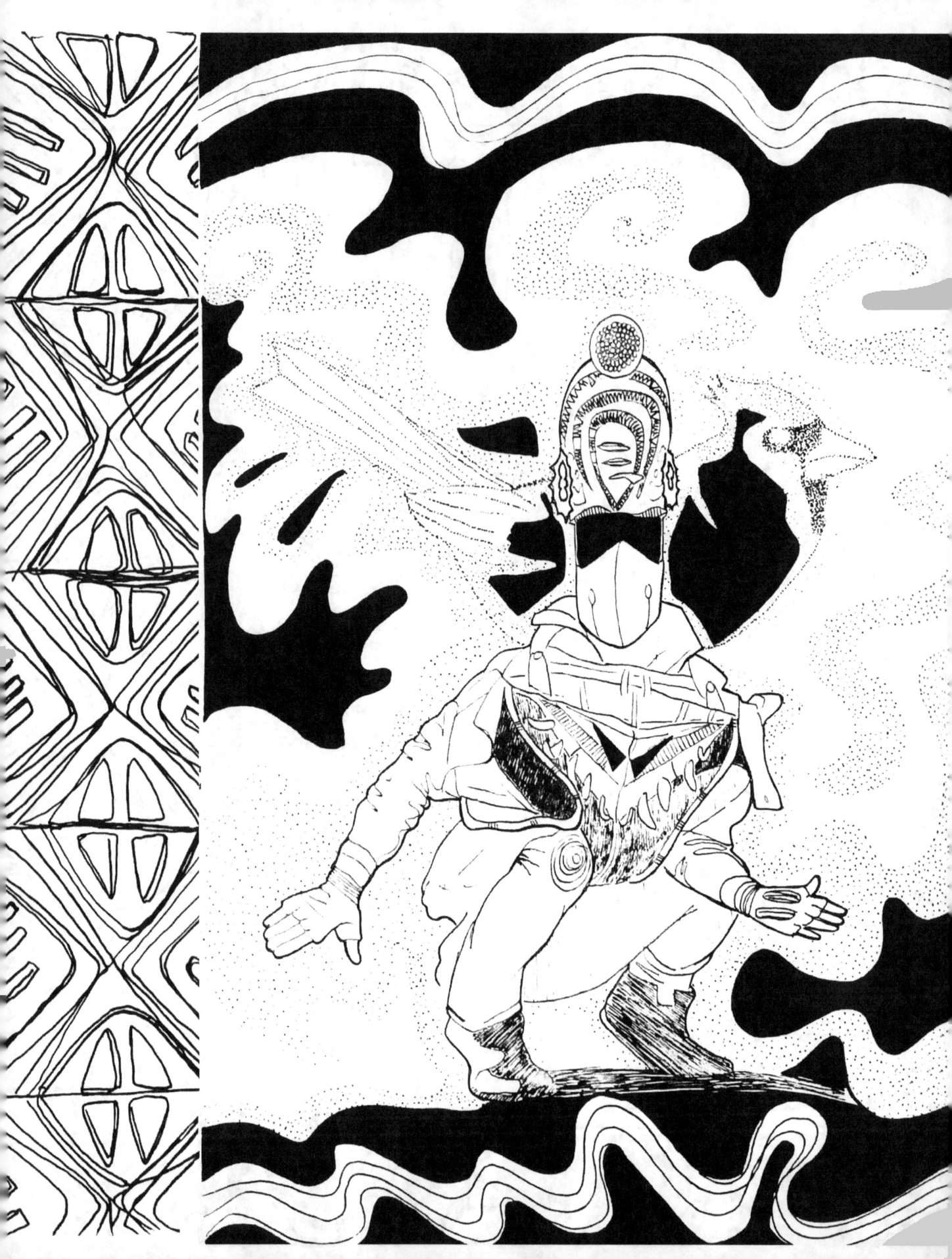

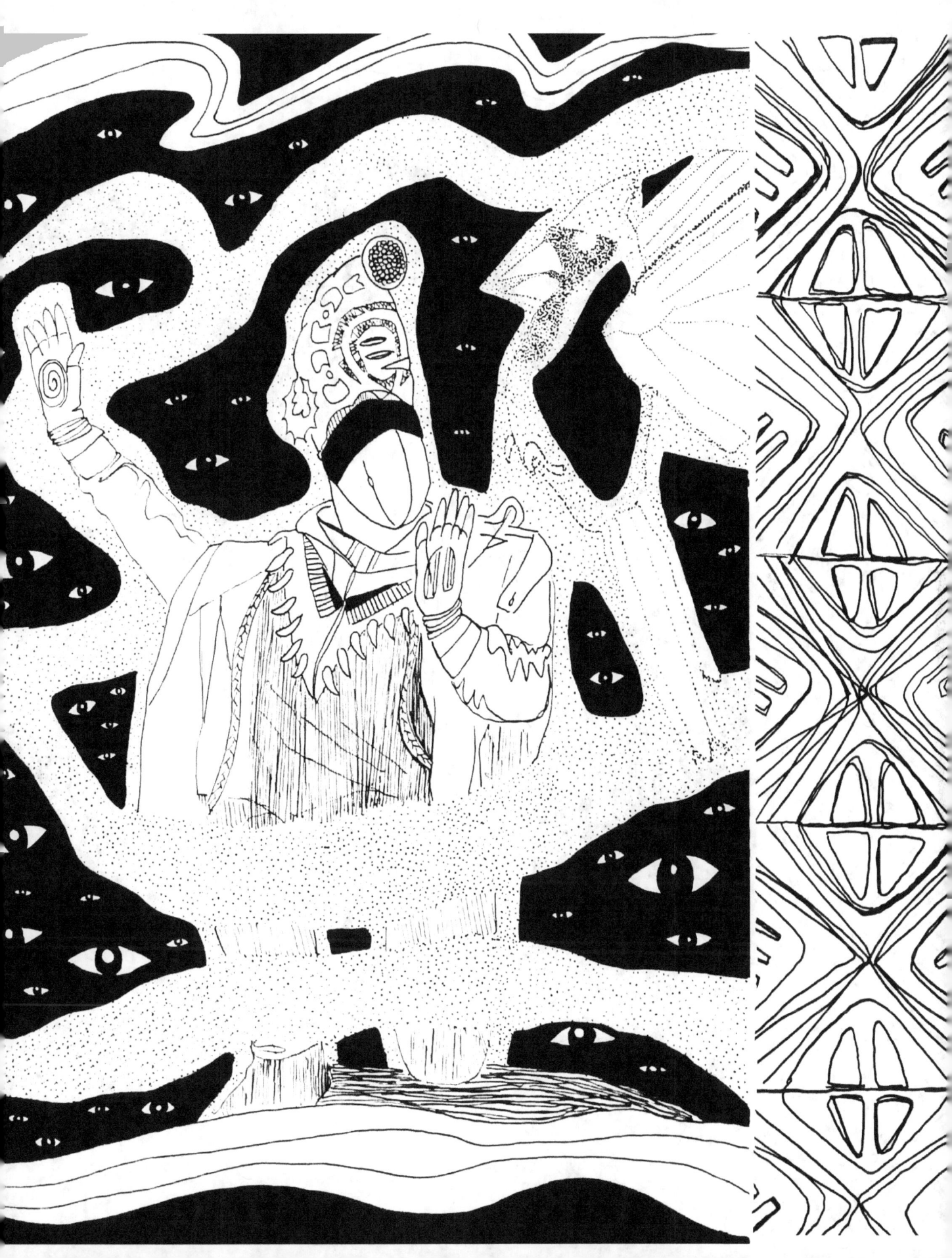

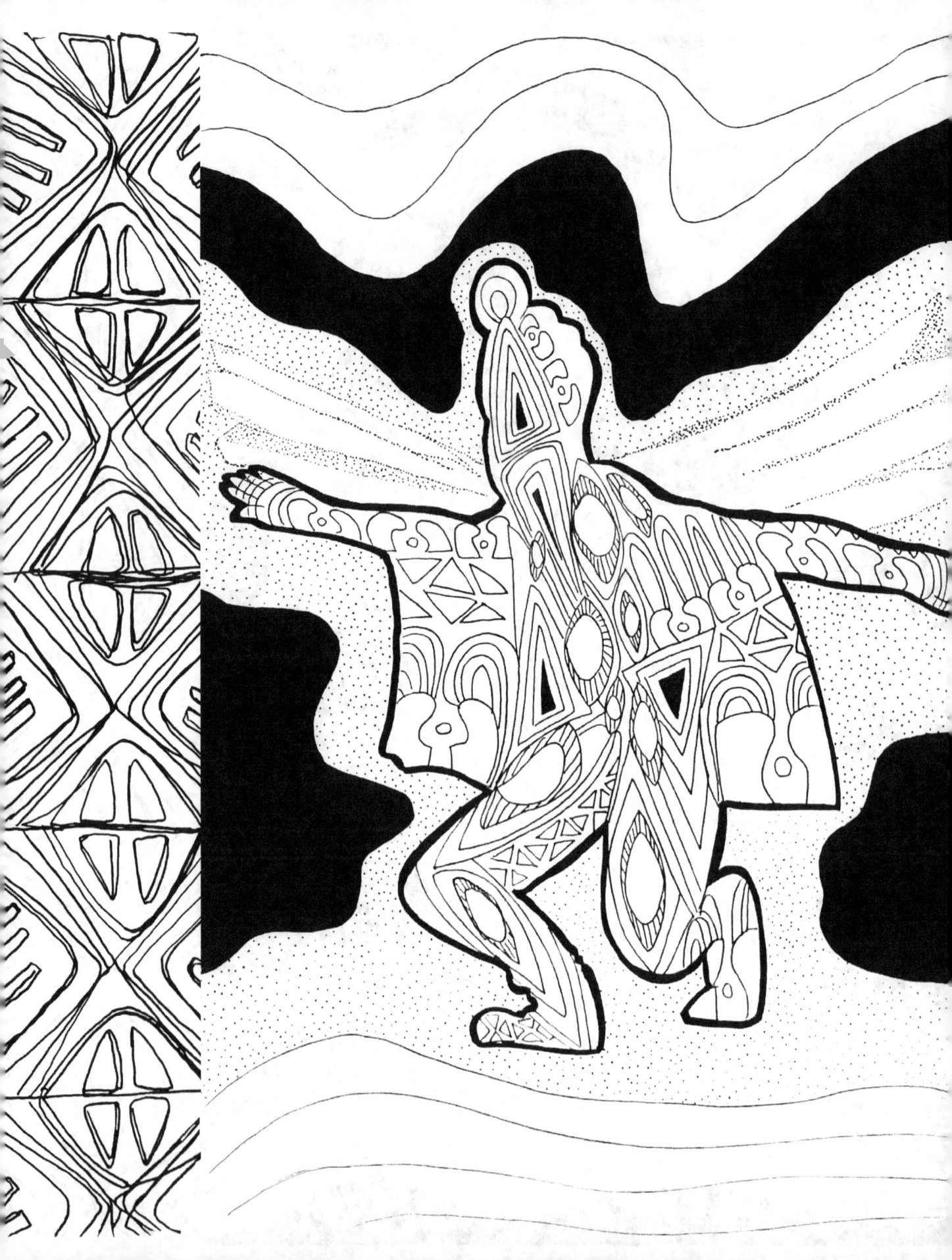

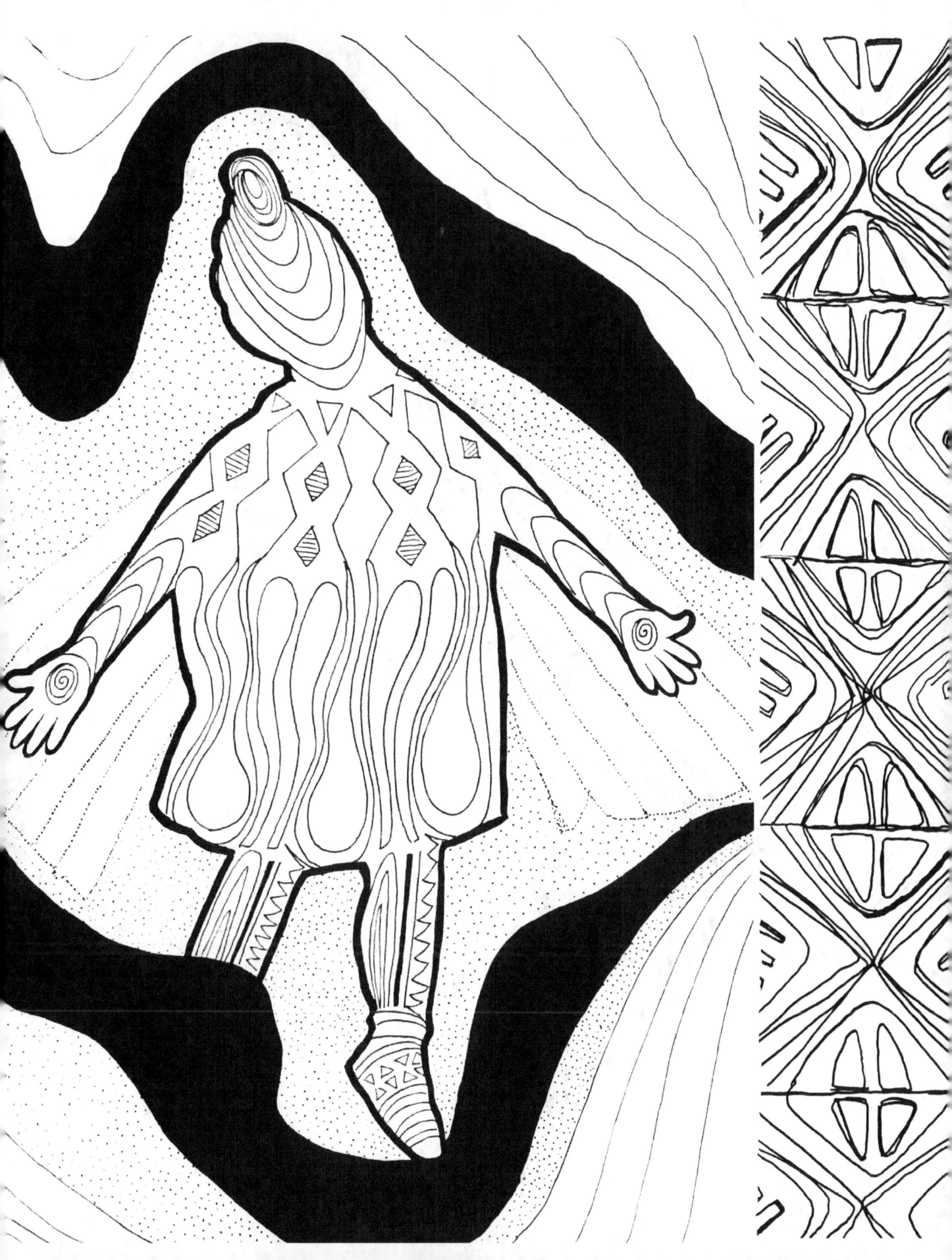

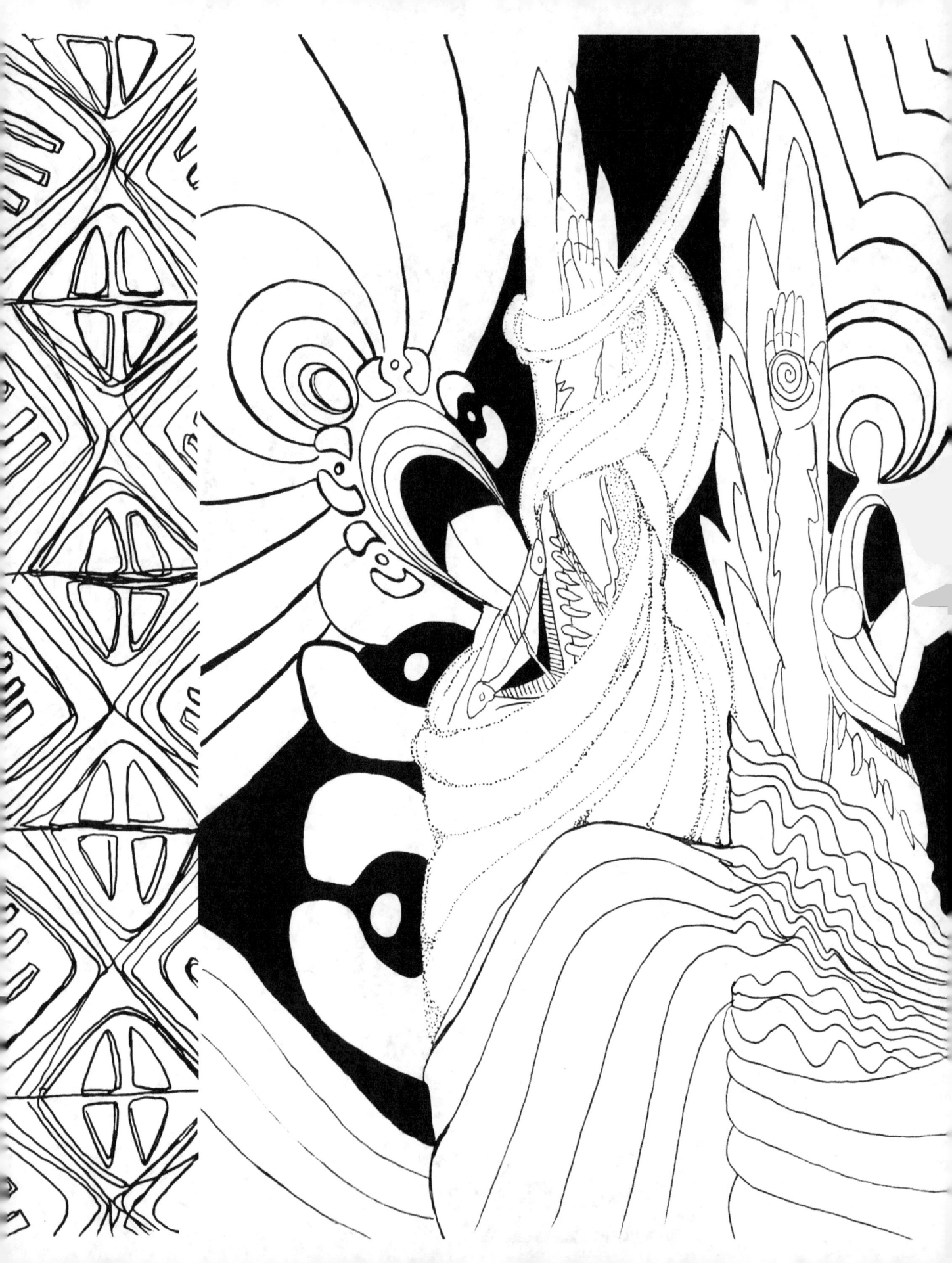

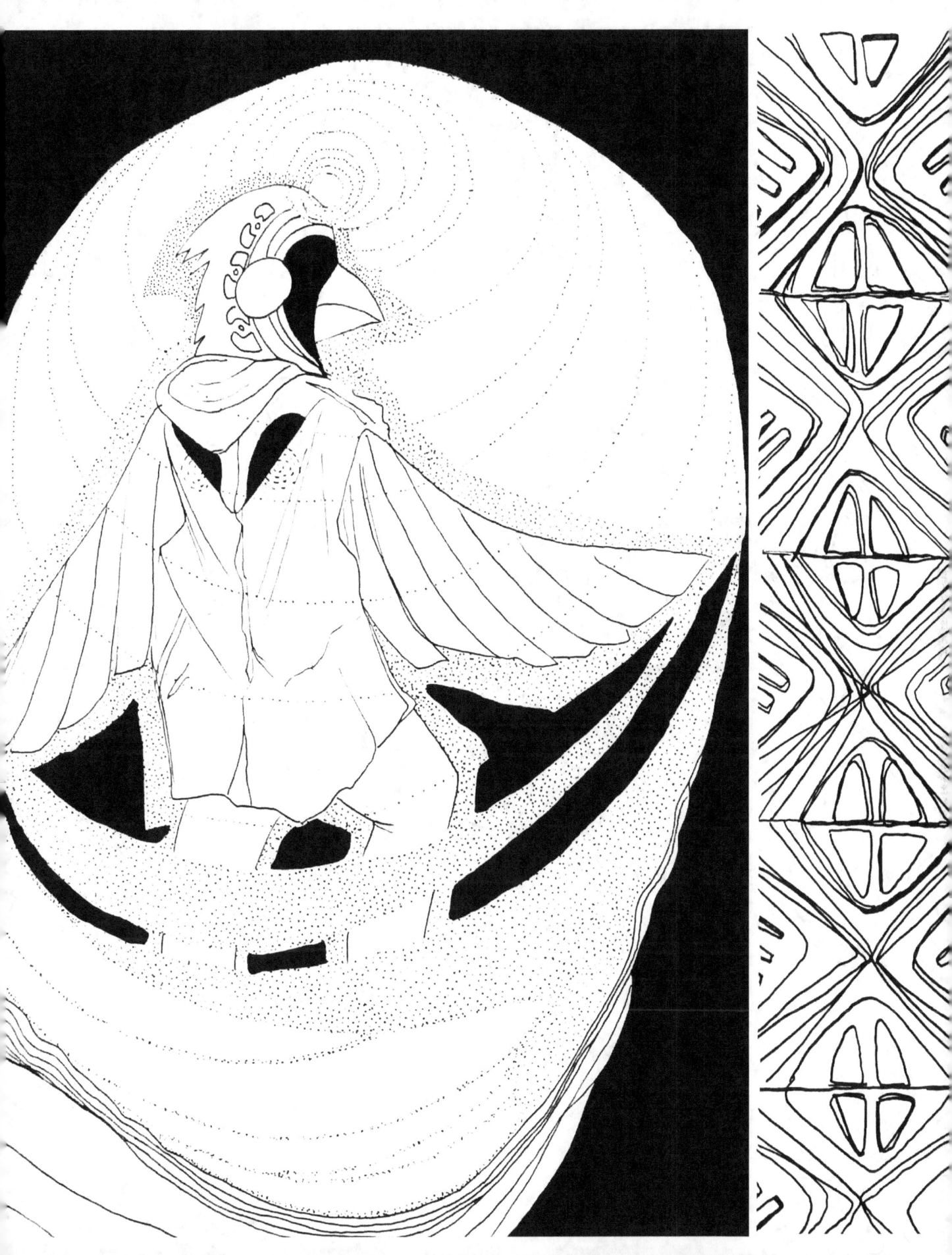

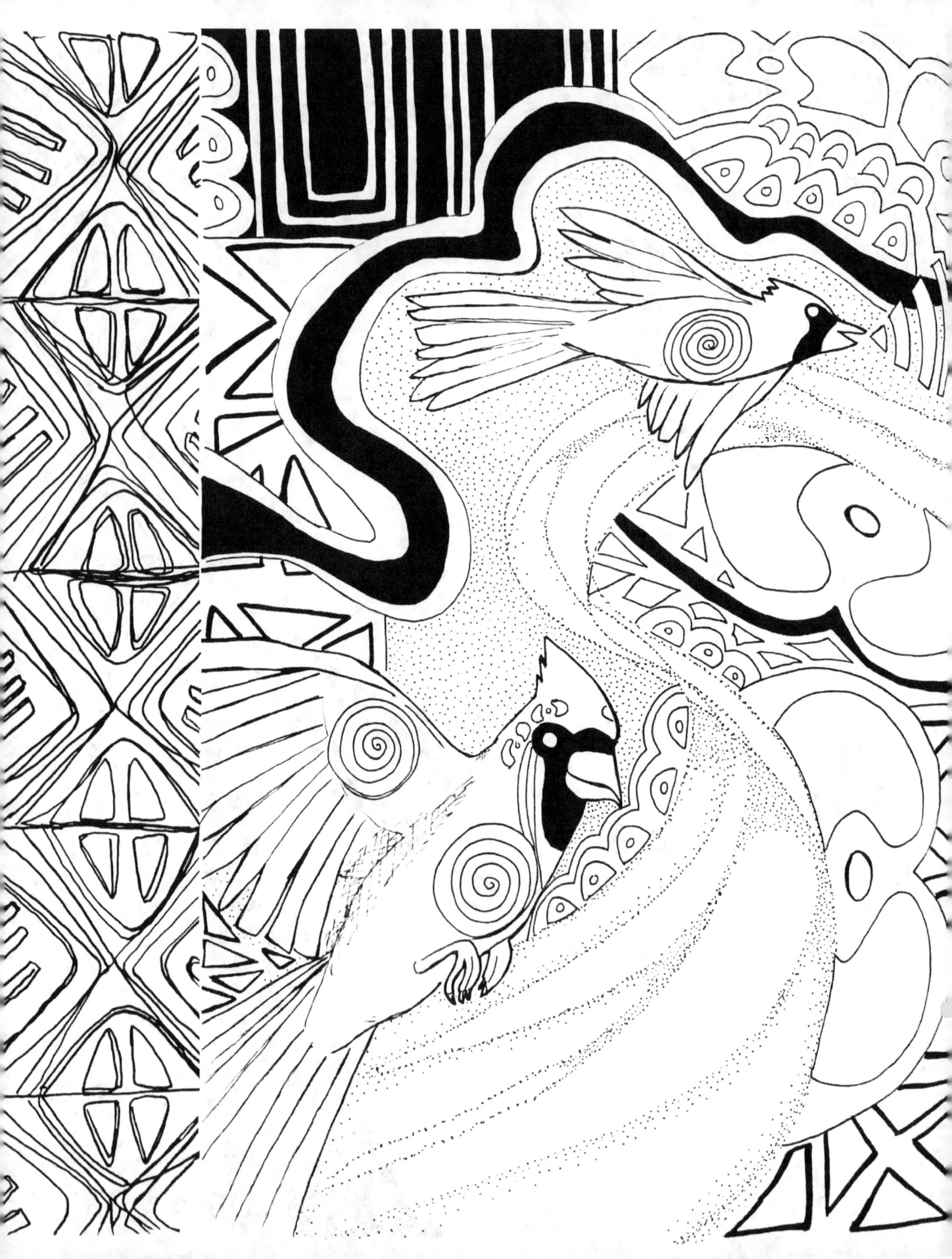

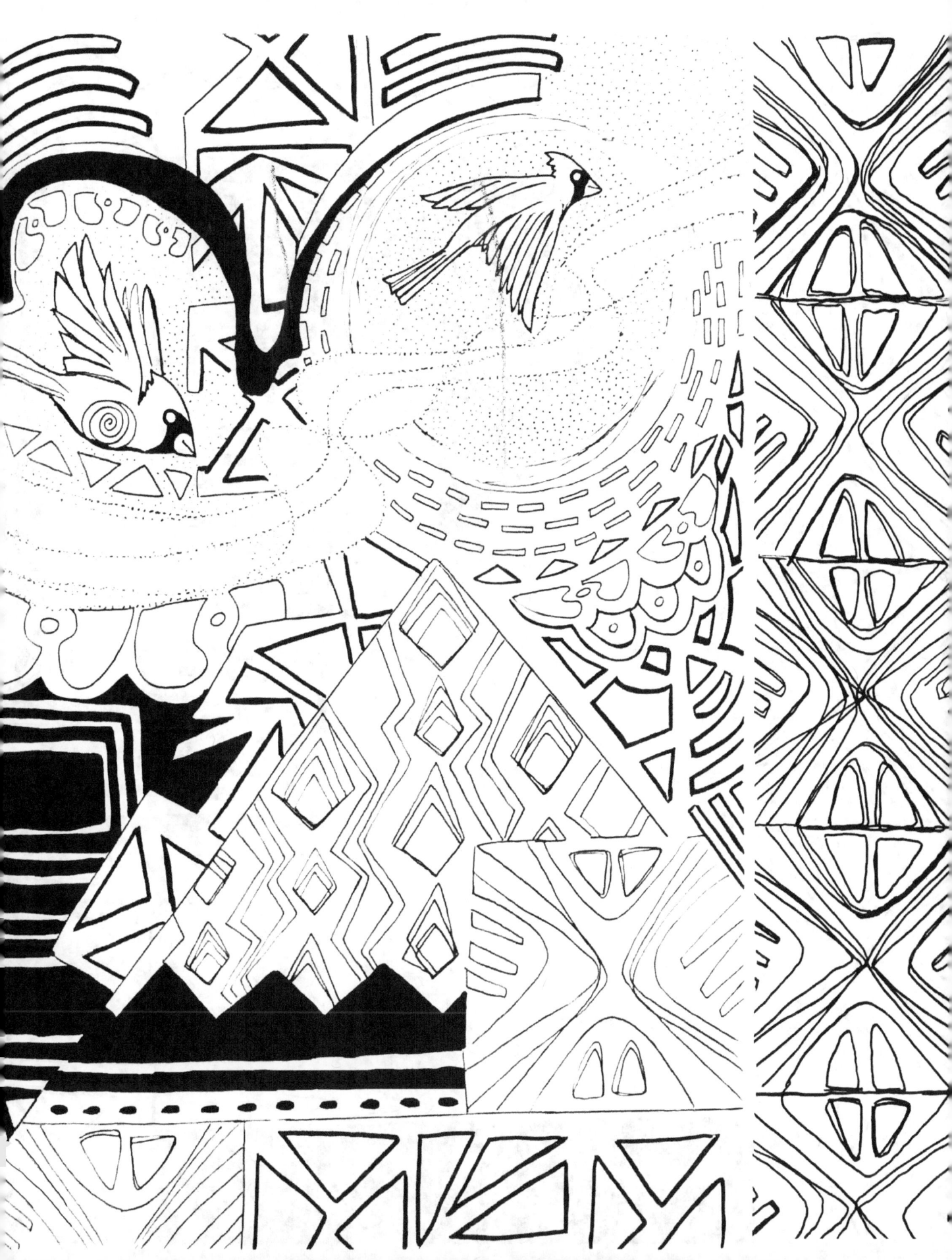

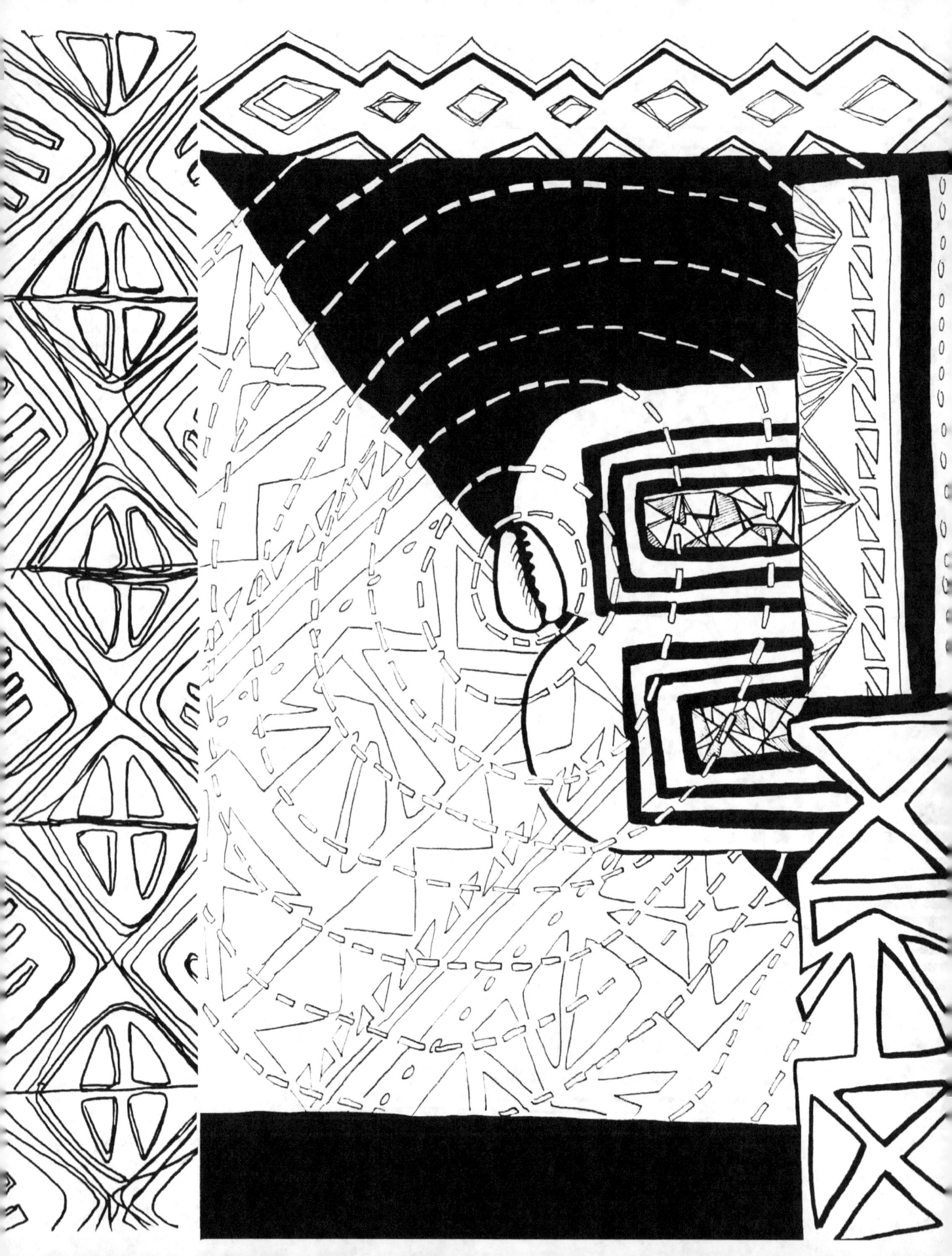

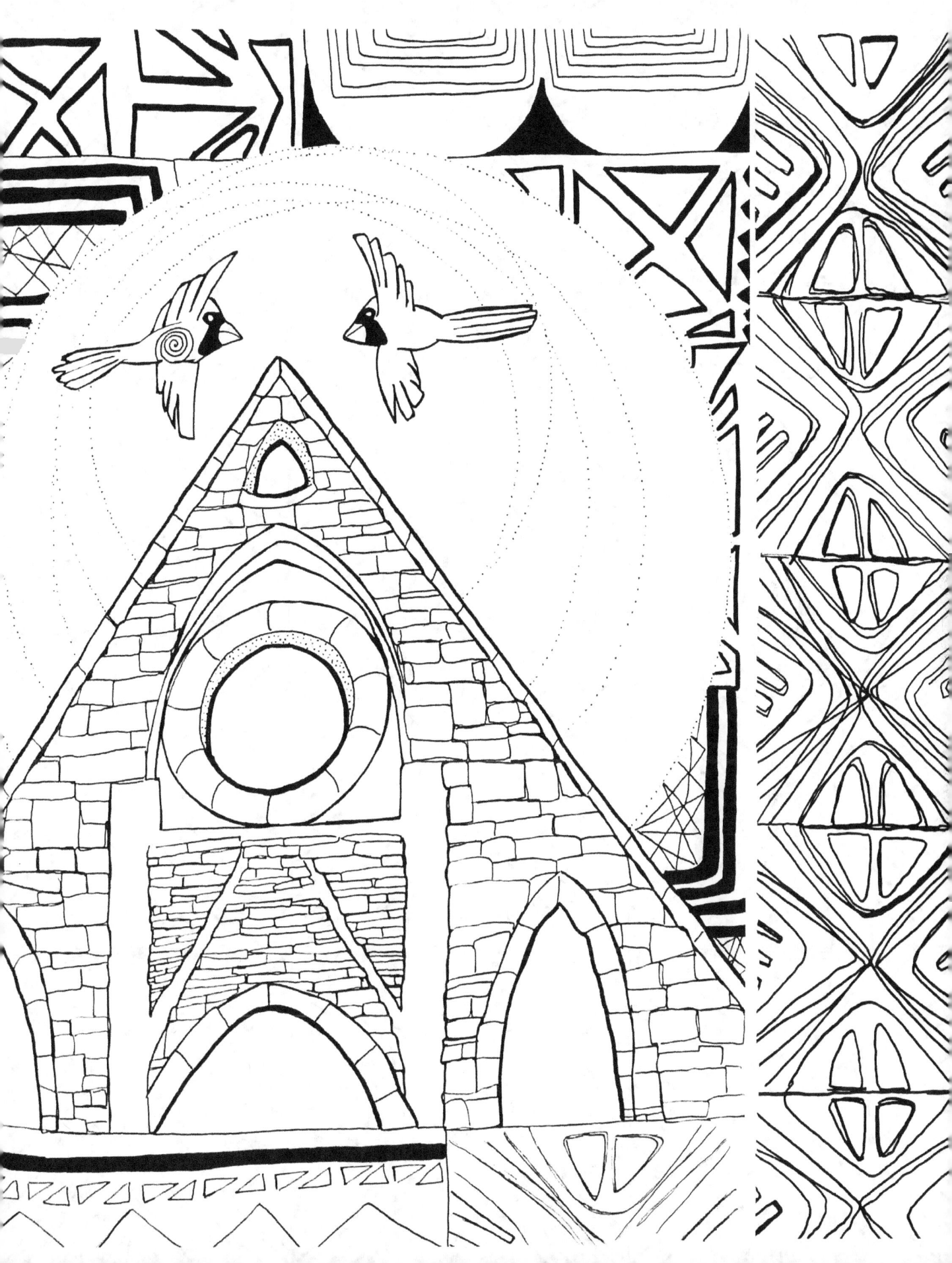

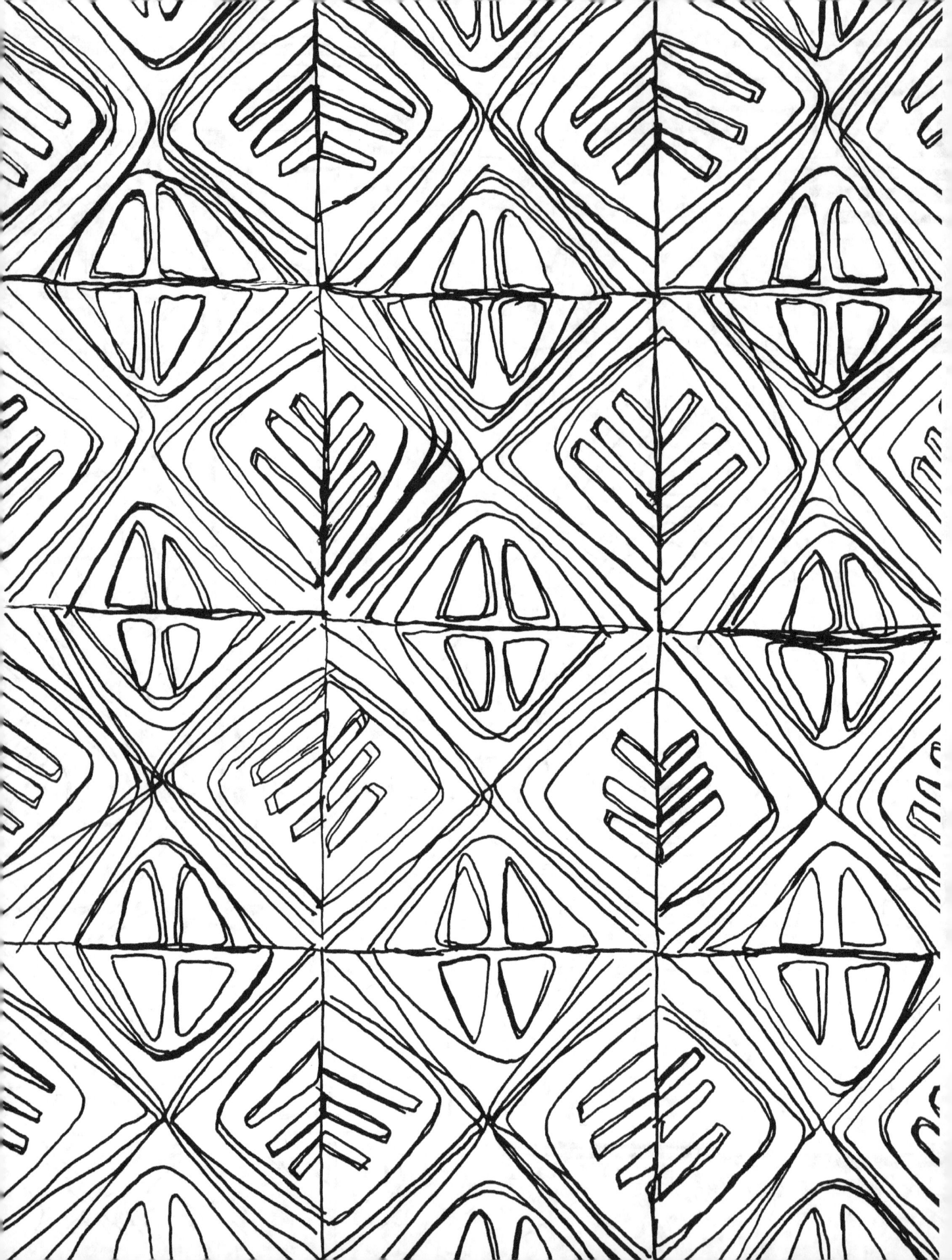

Draw **YOUR** hopeful future.